Dare 2B Wise

Joe White
Kelli Stuart

HOWARD BOOKS
A DIVISION OF SIMON & SCHUSTER
New York   London   Toronto   Sydney

Our purpose at Howard Books is to:

- *Increase faith* in the hearts of growing Christians
- *Inspire holiness* in the lives of believers
- *Instill hope* in the hearts of struggling people everywhere

Because He's coming again!

HOWARD
BOOKS

Published by Howard Books, a division of Simon & Schuster, Inc.
1230 Avenue of the Americas, New York, NY 10020
www.howardpublishing.com

Dare 2B Wise © 2004 by Joe White and Kelli Stuart

White, Joe, 1948-
   Dare 2B wise / Joe White and Kelli Stuart.
     p. cm.
   10 Digit ISBN: 1-58229-388-0; 13 Digit ISBN: 978-1-58229-388-2
   1. Bible. O.T. Proverbs--Devotional literature. 2. Christian teenagers--Prayer-books and devotions--English. 3. Family--Prayer-books and devotions--English. I. Title: Dare to be wise. II. Stuart, Kelli, 1978- III. Title.

BS1465.54.W49 2004
249--dc22

2004042485

11 10 9 8 7 6

Manufactured in the United States of America

For information regarding special discounts for bulk purchases, please contact: Simon & Schuster Special Sales at 1-800-456-6798 or business@simonandschuster.com.

Edited by Between the Lines
Interior design by Gabe Cardinale
Cover design by LinDee Loveland
Contributing writers: Joe Bednar, Roberta Bonnici, Melinda Booze, Lindsay Hill, Meredith Reed Knapp, Steve Lopez, Dan Mabery

About the Authors

 **Joe White:** Dr. James Dobson of Focus on the Family says that Joe White knows more about teenagers than anyone in North America. President of Kanakuk Kamps and founder of seven other summer camps, Joe has spoken at Promise Keepers, Focus on the Family radio, and NFL football and professional baseball chapels. He has authored fourteen books, including *FaithTraining* and the Gold Medallion Book of the Year for Teens, *Pure Excitement.* He and his wife, Debbie-Jo, live in Branson, Missouri, and have four grown children and two grandchildren.

Kelli Stuart: Co–author Kelli Stuart is a freelance writer and editor and is currently working on two non-fiction projects. Kelly lives in St. Louis, Missouri, where she and her husband, Lee, recently celebrated the birth of their first son, Sloan Alexander.

Dedication

To Trevor Mabery, Jack Herschend, and my dad—
the three wisest men I ever met.
—Joe White

To my parents, who daily modeled wisdom to me.
My father taught me that persistence and diligence lead to great reward (Proverbs 12:27; 13:4).
My mother taught me that kindness is far more respectable than whom you know,
what you look like, or what you do (Proverbs 11:16).
I am grateful to you both.
—Kelli Stuart

Contents

Introduction

My dad was a wise man. He'd say the funniest things to me sometimes, like:

"You don't have to; you get to."

"It doesn't hurt a fellow to hurt a little."

"It's a lot easier to borrow things than it is to give them back."

"It's funny how we do things for people who need it the least."

"Always be good to your mom."

Funny things? Yeah, because it's funny how those simple truths (and a million others) he taught me have stayed with me my whole life.

Daddy read the Bible and tried to live by it. Life for me isn't the same since he died. I miss his words, but mostly I miss his friendship.

When my two sons, Cooper and Brady, were in junior high and high school, I'd cook breakfast for them almost every time I was home. (Unfortunately, I travel a lot.) Before they went to bed at night, I took their breakfast order like I was a chef in some big restaurant. I offered a choice of French toast, pancakes of all kinds, juevos rancheros, bacon and eggs, or just a good ol' bowl of cereal. At the breakfast table, we'd open up the book of Proverbs, read a few verses, and talk about them. I learned that practice from my dad, and I tried to follow in his footsteps.

Next we would hold hands and pray, and then the tornado of teenage activity would sweep my sons out of the house. Those devotions were the best way we ever started our days together. Brady played basketball and Cooper played football, so our mornings were crazy—like yours—getting ready for sports and school. Some days they liked their dad and some days they didn't, but God was always our favorite, no matter what. Through thick and thin, we took time to seek his wisdom.

Brady and Cooper graduated from high school in love with God and best friends with their dad. It was definitely worth the priority in our scheduling to have devotions together. Now that they've graduated, I miss those times together like crazy.

I hope and pray the devotions in this book will bless your life too.

Joe White

The proverbs of Solomon son of David, king of Israel: for attaining wisdom and discipline; for understanding words of insight; for acquiring a disciplined and prudent life, doing what is right and just and fair; for giving prudence to the simple, knowledge and discretion to the young—let the wise listen and add to their learning, and let the discerning get guidance—for understanding proverbs and parables, the sayings and riddles of the wise.

—Proverbs 1:1–6

1. wise up

An old bumper sticker that was popular in Texas read, "If you don't have an oil well, get one!" The obvious joke was that everyone would like to have an oil well, but getting one is a lot easier said than done. The message of the book of Proverbs is similar: If you don't have wisdom, get some! But unlike the bumper sticker, the message of Proverbs is no joke. And unlike the humorous slogan, Proverbs doesn't tell you to get something—wisdom—without telling you how.

The highest goal you can set for yourself, the best use you can make of your time, and the smartest choice you can make in life is to follow the advice of Proverbs and get wisdom. But what is wisdom? The meaning of that word is fuzzy, isn't it? That's because people use the word wisdom to mean all sorts of different things.

In the Bible the word wisdom means the skill to live God's way. It comes through gaining understanding about how God wants you to live and then applying that understanding by putting it into practice in your daily life. If you do that over the course of your life, you'll be wise! And being wise is better than being rich, popular, famous, a great athlete, or any of the other earthly goals we set for ourselves.

So if I want to get wisdom, where do I start? Tomorrow we'll look at the first step on the exciting, lifelong journey of becoming wise.

discussion starters

1. What does wisdom mean to you? How is being wise different from being smart?
2. Why do you think it's important to God that we get wisdom?

lifeline

Pray that God will give you wisdom as you study the book of Proverbs and help you to apply the things you learn in your daily life.

The fear of the LORD is the beginning of knowledge, but fools despise wisdom and discipline.

—*Proverbs 1:7*

2. start with God

If you want to be wise, you must start with God. In fact, you must not only start with God but finish with God and walk with God every step of the way. If you start anywhere else, you'll never be wise—no matter how hard you try. The only wisdom worth having is God's wisdom. And he gives us this wisdom as we diligently seek him. Seeking him basically means two things: (1) learning how he wants us to live, and (2) doing our best to become more like him.

Today's verse tells us that the "fear of the LORD" is the first step in our quest for wisdom. This starting point is so essential to gaining wisdom that Solomon emphasizes it again later: "The fear of the LORD is the beginning of wisdom" (Proverbs 9:10). But what is the "fear of the LORD"? Does it mean we should be afraid of God? No.

In the Bible "fear of the LORD" means a proper respect for who God is and who we are in relation to him. It means understanding that God is the all-powerful, righteous Creator of the universe and that we are sinners who are not even worthy to stand in his presence. And yet God loved us so much that he sent his only Son, Jesus Christ, to die on the cross for our sins (John 3:16).

If we admit to God that we're sinners—that we've fallen short of his standard of perfection—and accept the sacrifice Jesus made for us on the cross, he will actually come into our hearts and live inside us. We will be new creations (2 Corinthians 5:17), righteous in God's sight and bound for eternal life in heaven. Salvation is a free gift from God that we can't earn by doing good things or by being good. We must simply acknowledge that we are sinners unworthy to enter heaven, and we must accept the free gift of salvation that God offers us through Christ.

When we understand how lost we were before God saved us—when we truly understand the eternal death from which God saved us and the eternal life for which he saved us—we'll respond to him with awe, reverence, worship, and obedience. Then we'll have the "fear of the LORD" and be ready to start out on our quest for wisdom.

discussion starters

1. Have you accepted Jesus Christ as your Savior? If so, thank God for his awesome gift of salvation! How has this gift made a difference in your life?
2. If not, what questions or fears do you have that might keep you from accepting him? Why not pray and accept his free gift of salvation right now?
3. What does the "fear of the Lord" mean to you? How do you think being a Christian (accepting Jesus' gift of salvation) helps you to fear the Lord?

lifeline

Memorize John 3:16: "God so loved the world that he gave his one and only Son, that whoever believes in him shall not perish but have eternal life." If you've already memorized this verse, why not *share* it with someone who needs to hear it this week?

3. bad company

My son, if sinners entice you, do not give in to them. If they say, "Come along with us; let's lie in wait for someone's blood, let's waylay some harmless soul; . . . my son, do not go along with them, do not set foot on their paths; for their feet rush into sin, they are swift to shed blood. . . . These men lie in wait for their own blood; they waylay only themselves! Such is the end of all who go after ill-gotten gain; it takes away the lives of those who get it.

—Proverbs 1:10–11, 15–16, 18–19

Sarah was new at school. Her family had just moved to the city where her dad had taken a new job. She had been popular at her old school, but she didn't have any friends at this new one. Then one day a group of kids invited her to sit with them at lunch. She couldn't believe they would pick her to hang out with. They were some of the most popular kids in the school! But these kids were different from her old friends. Her old friends had been Christians, and she always felt good about herself when she was with them. Sarah didn't think her new friends were bad people, but they had reputations for throwing wild parties and getting into trouble.

Sarah wanted to do the right thing, but she also *really* wanted to be accepted at her new school. So she started hanging out with this new group of friends. She stayed on the fringes at first, just watching and not participating in things she knew were wrong. But as time passed, Sarah's mind-set started to change. "Maybe smoking pot just this once won't hurt me," she thought. So she tried it. Next it was "I really like Bobby. Maybe it wouldn't be so wrong for me to sleep with him. After all, he says he loves me, and all the other girls are sleeping with their boyfriends." So she did. She felt terrible about herself, but her need to be accepted was strong.

A few months later, Sarah sat on her bed and wept. She looked in the mirror and didn't recognize herself anymore. She didn't remember where the line between right and wrong was or when she had crossed it, but she knew she had. She was amazed at how easy it had been to follow her new friends, inch by inch, into a lifestyle she knew was displeasing to God, her parents, and herself.

Do you want to be wise? The Bible says to hang out with wise friends. Foolish friends may promise to make you popular and happy, but they *will* bring you down in the end. Every time. Wise friends, on the other hand, will build you up and help you make good choices. They'll support you against the pressure to do things you know are wrong, and they'll help you feel truly good about who you are. Choosing wise friends is one of the wisest choices you can make.

discussion starters

1. Are your best friends wise or unwise people? Can you think of a wise person at your school whom you'd like to get to know better?
2. Think of a time when hanging around the wrong kind of friends got you into trouble. How can you avoid that happening again?

lifeline

Ask God to bring wise friends into your life. **Consider** why you hang out with your current group. Are you trying to please others or please God?

Wisdom calls aloud in the street, she raises her voice in the public squares; at the head of the noisy streets she cries out, in the gateways of the city she makes her speech.

—Proverbs 1:20–21

4. street preacher

"TURN . . . FROM . . . SIN!" the street preacher booms in a voice you can hear blocks away. Then he does a little hip-hop, perfected over years of practice, and lands facing the other way. "TURN . . . TO . . . GOD!" he booms again, and then starts over.

"TURN . . . FROM . . . SIN!" (hop) "TURN . . . TO . . . GOD!" (hop)

"TURN . . . FROM . . . SIN!" (hop) "TURN . . . TO . . . GOD!" (hop)

Day after day, month after month, and year after year, the preacher stands on the same busy street corner in weather-beaten clothes with an even more weather-beaten Bible in his hands and cries out to the masses of people scurrying by: "TURN FROM SIN! TURN TO GOD!"

Most people pass by without listening to him. They think he's crazy—a religious nut. Besides, they have more important things to do than listen to some guy yelling like a lunatic. But once in a while, once in a long while, somebody stops. And listens. And walks away changed. And that's why the street preacher keeps coming back.

People search for wisdom everywhere: in distant caves and deserts; high in the Himalaya Mountains; or through drugs or magic crystals or, someday, by traveling through space to other worlds. But the Bible reveals an awesome and encouraging truth: Wisdom isn't hiding. Wisdom is a street preacher, standing on every corner, crying out with a passion to help anyone who will listen.

"Well, I can't *hear* wisdom," you might say. "Wisdom isn't *really* a street preacher standing on a corner." And you're right. The picture of wisdom as a street preacher in Proverbs is a personification—

it takes an abstract concept you can't see or hear and presents it as if it were a person. So, how do you hear wisdom? The key is found in Proverbs 2:6: "The LORD gives wisdom, and from his mouth come knowledge and understanding." Listening to wisdom is listening to God.

My dad always seemed to know what God wanted him to do. So one day I asked him, "Does God talk to you?"

"Some people say God talks to them," he answered. "Maybe he does, and maybe he doesn't. I can just say he's never talked to me in a voice I can hear. But God talks to me in other ways. I read my Bible and pray and confess my sins to him. Then I ask him to show me the right choices to make in life. If I'm willing to obey him and make those choices, he guides me by opening the doors for choices he wants me to make and closing the doors on others. That's how God 'talks' to me."

My dad stopped and listened when the street preacher talked, and it made him the wisest person I've ever known. Most people won't listen to wisdom. Will you?

discussion starters

1. How can you listen to what wisdom has to say? Are you willing to do that?
2. What are some reasons people don't listen to wisdom? What are some of the dangers of ignoring wisdom's advice?

lifeline

Pray that God will help you listen to his wisdom and follow his wise advice.

How long will you simple ones love your simple ways? How long will mockers delight in mockery and fools hate knowledge?

—*Proverbs 1:22*

5. all the world's a stage

Proverbs is like a play with three main characters that appear throughout the book: the Wise, the Fool, and the Simple. The Wise listens to God's advice and follows it consistently throughout his life so he becomes more and more like Jesus. Sure he makes mistakes, but he's quick to get back on track and move forward, doing what God wants him to do.

On the other end of the spectrum is the Fool (and his nasty cousin the Mocker). The Fool has heard what God has to say but has rejected it. Instead he follows his own path, which constantly gets him into trouble. What's worse, the Fool isn't content just to make his own bad choices; he tries to bring others down with him.

Between these two extremes is the Simple. He isn't bad or stupid; he's just inexperienced. He has just walked onto the stage and hasn't yet made his choice to become Wise or to become a Fool.

The drama of Proverbs is real. It's being acted out in the world around us every day. The Wise, the Fool, and the Simple are recognizable characters you meet everywhere. In fact, you may be one of those characters—or some combination of them.

Wisdom calls out to all three of these characters. To the Wise she says, "Keep it up! Becoming like Jesus is a lifelong process, and you can always be wiser. There's no standing still in the Christian life, so if you stop moving forward, you'll slide backward. Press on!" To the Fool wisdom cries, "Turn away from your foolish lifestyle! There's still time! Listen to me and become wise!" And to the Simple wisdom says, "You have a choice! Please listen to what I say. The path of the Fool will destroy you, but the path of the Wise will give you abundant life. Choose to be wise!"

The good news is, if you don't like your role in this play, you can change it. Even if you've been the Fool for many years, you can start becoming Wise today. If you're Simple (and most of us are, at least in part) you can choose to become Wise. Regardless of where you are today, Proverbs is full of advice on how to move into a better, godlier role in the play of life.

discussion starters

1. Which of the three main characters in Proverbs—the Wise, the Simple, or the Fool—are you most like?
2. How do you think the Simple can avoid becoming the Fool and become Wise instead?

lifeline

Set this goal for yourself today: I will not reject God's wisdom and be a fool. I will listen and be wise.

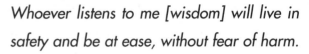

Whoever listens to me [wisdom] will live in safety and be at ease, without fear of harm.

—Proverbs 1:33

6. safe and at ease

I still remember the first time I lied to my mom. (I was all of five years old.) I also remember the first time I stole candy from a store. (I was seven.) And the time I crawled over the fence and snuck into the football game without buying a ticket. And I remember the first time, in my stupid youth, that I cursed God and disobeyed his commands.

I wasn't a criminal, but I was (and still am) so far from perfect I couldn't even spell the word! I knew enough about God from church and from my parents that my conscience *killed* me every time I willfully sinned against him. I was in constant fear of the "harm" that would come to me if I got caught, and I certainly did not feel "safe" and "at ease"—the promises from today's verse for those who listen to God.

Fortunately, Jesus came into my heart. Fortunately, he forgave me. Fortunately, he taught me how to get it right. The clean conscience that his forgiveness gave me and the peaceful conscience following his ways have given me the feeling of "safety" and "ease" promised.

There is no sin on earth worth the price of an uneasy conscience. A clear conscience may just very well be the best gift we could ever give ourselves.

discussion starters

1. Why is an uneasy conscience so persistent?
2. How does obeying Jesus help us live in safety and be at ease?
3. Is there anything in your conscience that needs a good spiritual cleansing today?

lifeline

Write down the things in your life that make you feel uneasy and worried about possible consequences. Then *write out* a plan to bring your life in line with God's Word.

7. the treasure of wisdom

My son, if you accept my words and store up my commands within you, turning your ear to wisdom and applying your heart to understanding, and if you call out for insight and cry aloud for understanding, and if you look for it as for silver and search for it as for hidden treasure, then you will understand the fear of the LORD and find the knowledge of God.

—*Proverbs 2:1–5*

Solomon could have been a twenty-first-century Bill Gates—he had it all! The stock market was good. The Dow Jones was rolling. The market was bullish. The girls were beautiful, and dates were plentiful. He could have asked for anything; his horizon was broad. But besides great wealth, Solomon had great insight. Given the chance, he asked for the one thing he knew would benefit him most: wisdom.

- Wisdom is the ability to discern good and evil, to see things as God sees them. Solomon treasured wisdom above all else, and God blessed him beyond measure.
- Wisdom helps you know when admiration for good looks turns into lust.
- Wisdom shows you when your quest for excellence turns into perfectionism.
- Wisdom identifies music, movies, and entertainment as pleasing to God or as messages from the jaws of hell.

- Wisdom tells you whom to date, love, and marry—the one who will put a smile in your heart rather than the one who will someday leave your life in ruins.
- Wisdom polarizes your spiritual sunglasses to filter out Satan's tricky, conniving appeal and filter in the mind of Christ.

It has been said that a person will forfeit long-term dreams for short-term pleasures. But wisdom will guide your short-term desires so your long-term dreams can come true.

discussion starters

1. Do you know anyone your age who shows unusual wisdom? How can you tell?
2. Do you think you can know the wise decision ahead of time and still make a foolish decision when the time comes? Why? How can you keep from doing that?

lifeline

Pray that, above all else, God gives you abundant wisdom.

Walk in the ways of good men and keep to the paths of the righteous. For the upright will live in the land, and the blameless will remain in it.

—*Proverbs 2:20–21*

8. walking in integrity

My mom made a big mistake in my ninth-grade year when she asked my brother Bill (who lived life a little on the edge) what size engine she needed to order for her new Chevrolet Impala. "Oh, Mom, you need one of those 350-horse-power, 409-cubic-inch Chevys." Right.

When I grew up in Texas, the legal driving age was fourteen. Needless to say, I loved to get in the Impala and let that baby run! But alas, on my first date one Friday night after a football game, my free-spirited drive came to a screeching halt when big, red, flashing highway-patrol lights appeared in the rearview mirror. When the officer approached the car with his ticket book, I really didn't have anything to say. I knew I was guilty. And the seventy-dollar ticket would be nothing compared with facing my dad and losing my driver's license for a month. I felt like I would have given anything to keep him from learning of my run-in with the law.

How thankful I am that Jesus came to earth and died on the cross for our sins. I'm so glad I don't have to face God carrying the guilt of breaking his laws! Losing my driver's license for a month was nothing compared to what spending eternity in hell would be. Thanks be to God, I don't have to face that judgment because Jesus faced it on my behalf.

Just the same, it is my duty, my honor, my job to walk in integrity everyday. Because of what Jesus did for us, we must dedicate ourselves to walking in even higher integrity just to say "thank you, Jesus."

discussion starters

1. Have you ever done something that made you feel so guilty it kept you from enjoying life—even before you were found out?
2. How can your thankfulness to Jesus' sacrifice motivate you to walk in integrity?

lifeline

Ask God to help you live a blameless life so that when you die, you won't have to face him with guilt or fear of punishment.

My son, do not forget my teaching, but keep my commands in your heart, for they will prolong your life many years and bring you prosperity.

—Proverbs 3:1–2

9. live long and prosper

Dan's father was one of the finest Christian men he had ever known. He was a fantastic role model for his children and a wise leader in the church. He had Jesus' knack for treating everyone he met as though he or she were the only person who mattered. Most importantly, he lived every day of his life for Jesus, storing up treasures in heaven rather than on earth.

So when his dad died in a plane crash on the way home from a Christian men's retreat in Montana, when he was only fifty-one years old, Dan struggled with the principle in Proverbs 3:1–2. Doesn't the Bible say people who live God's way will live long and prosperous lives? Then Dan remembered an important truth. Proverbs are principles, not promises. They're statements about how things usually work. They describe principles that apply most of the time, although there are exceptions—like with his dad.

But the fact that proverbs aren't promises doesn't mean they aren't true statements. Those who remember God's teaching and keep his commands usually will live long lives and prosper. So if you want to dramatically increase the probability that you'll live a long and prosperous life, live God's way.

Why do people who follow God's commands often live longer? Because God's commands are good for us. When you were a little kid, your parents probably told you not to play in the street. At the time you might have thought they were being unfair, even mean. But as you got older, you realized they restricted your play area because they loved you. If you don't play in the street, you'll live longer. In the same way, God knows that sin is dangerous. It may seem fun to us, and Satan tries to trick us into believing that God made rules just to keep us from having a good time. But the truth is that God's rules are designed to help us live long, healthy, exciting lives.

Proverbs 3:1–2 also says people who follow God's commands enjoy prosperity. By prosperity the Bible doesn't mean that each of us should have a million bucks and a Mercedes Benz and that if we don't, we must lack faith. It means that if we devote our best energy to serving Jesus, he'll take care of our needs. If we're living for him, we can stop worrying about money, food, and clothes—he's got it covered. As the Bible says, "Seek first his kingdom and his righteousness, and all these things will be given to you as well" (Matthew 6:33).

discussion starters

1. What are some of God's commands that will help you live longer?
2. Do you think it's wrong for a Christian to have a lot of money?
3. Does the answer to that question depend on what the Christian does with that money? (Hint: See Matthew 25:14–30.)

lifeline

Focus on living God's way, and he'll take care of the rest!

Trust in the LORD with all your heart and lean not on your own understanding; in all your ways acknowledge him, and he will make your paths straight.

—Proverbs 3:5–6

10. w.w.y.d.

A few years ago, thousands of teens and kids across America wore wristbands to school that said, simply, W.W.J.D. The letters stand for a question: What would Jesus do? The point was to encourage young people, as they faced tough decisions in their lives, to ask that very important question: What would Jesus do in this situation?

What a great idea! We should all follow the advice on that wristband and ask ourselves what Jesus would do if he faced the same tough decisions we face. But through prayer, we can ask an even better question: W.W.Y.D. We can ask Jesus directly, "What would you do in this situation?" That's the point of Proverbs 3:5–6, which is one of the best-known passages in the Bible. It tells us to consult God when we face challenges and difficult decisions in life.

The Bible teaches a very important truth: When we accept Christ as our savior, we become new creations (2 Corinthians 5:17) with a new, sinless nature inside. Jesus lives in us and gives us power to make right choices. Unfortunately, this side of heaven, we also still have the power to make wrong choices. In fact, if we trust ourselves to make good decisions rather than asking God what we should do, we often will make the wrong choices. That's why it's crucial to consult God "in all your ways" rather than leaning "on your own understanding."

If we make a habit of asking God's advice before making important decisions, and if we follow that advice, he will give us lives that are truly worth living—full of joy, accomplishment, and exciting challenges. He will keep us on the right track toward the goal he has set for us, which is what Proverbs means when it says, "he will make your paths straight." If we ask God what we should do, and then do what he says, we can't go wrong!

discussion starters

1. Why is it dangerous to rely on yourself when you face tough decisions rather than asking God's advice?
2. Since God doesn't answer aloud when you ask him for advice, what are some ways he shows you what he wants you to do?
3. What decisions are you facing right now that you should ask God's advice about?

lifeline

Memorize Proverbs 3:5–6 and *pray* that God will help you do what it says.

Honor the LORD with your wealth, with the firstfruits of all your crops; then your barns will be filled to overflowing, and your vats will brim over with new wine.

—Proverbs 3:9–10

11. give to get

Jack, Ben, and Melissa are walking down the street. At the exact same moment, they see three brand-new, crisp thousand-dollar bills lying on the ground. Each picks one up. "Wow," Jack says. "I'm going to buy a thousand lottery tickets and get rich quick!"

Ben says, "I've been needing a new bike for my paper route. I can buy it and still have enough money left over to do whatever I want!"

Melissa says, "First, I'm going to put one hundred dollars in the offering plate at church. Then I'll ask God how I should use the nine hundred left over."

"What are you, nuts?" Jack exclaims. "You just found a thousand dollars, and you want to give part of it away? That's your money."

But Melissa understands an important principle from the book of Proverbs: God owns all the money in the world. Any money he lets us have is a gift from him. He still owns it; we just manage it for him. The Bible calls Christians, as managers of God's money, "stewards."

When we get money, God expects us to be wise stewards of the money he's entrusted us with and give part of it back to him. In fact, he expects us to give him the *first* part of it—not whatever is left over after we buy what we want. This doesn't make sense to people who don't understand why we would give money away instead of keeping it for ourselves. But if we give the first and best of all we have back to God, trusting him to take care of our needs, he will give it back to us many times over.

Giving the first part of our money back to God isn't something he wants us to do only if we feel like it. He demands it. In fact, did you know God says we're robbing him if we don't return to him the first part of all the money we get? In Malachi 3, God says we're stealing from him if we don't give him the tithes and offerings—the "firstfruits" of our wealth. But he also makes a promise: If we honor him with the first part of our money, he will give back to us far more than we give him. "'Bring the whole tithe [that is, the first tenth] into the storehouse, that there may be food in my house. Test me in this,' says the LORD Almighty, 'and see if I will not throw open the floodgates of heaven and pour out so much blessing that you will not have room enough for it'" (Malachi 3:10).

If you want to be wise, honor God with the first and best part of your money. It's hard at first, but once you start seeing how faithful God is, how he gives back to you much more than you give him, giving becomes a joy.

discussion starters

1. Now that you understand that God owns everything, how should you use your money differently than you do now?
2. God calls us to manage his money wisely, but he also calls us to be wise stewards of the time and talents he's given us. How can you be a wise steward of your time and talents?

lifeline

Next time you get money, *give* the first 10 percent of it back to God. Then watch him work!

Do not withhold good from those who deserve it, when it is in your power to act. Do not say to your neighbor, "Come back later; I'll give it tomorrow"—when you now have it with you.

—Proverbs 3:27–28

12. not my problem

"Help me," Lucy said weakly. "Help me, please." She staggered along the side of the road, using her one good arm to flag down passing cars. She had just had a terrible accident on her bicycle, which left her bruised and bleeding and with a broken collarbone. "Surely someone will stop and help me," she thought.

A doctor drove by in a BMW and saw her waving for help. "I'd like to help her out," he thought, "but I already have a bunch of patients waiting in my office. I can't keep them waiting too long or they'll go home, and then I couldn't take care of them. After all, the woman probably wasn't watching where she was going." He tried not to make eye contact with her as he passed by.

Then a lawyer drove by in a Lexus. "I'd better not get involved," she thought. "What if I tried to help her and just made her worse? She'd sue me!" The lawyer passed by too. Lucy was getting weaker.

A pastor drove by in a Hyundai. He slowed down and leaned out his window. "I'll pray for you, friend!" he said with a smile . . . and drove on by.

Lucy was losing hope when a homeless man walked by. He was on his way to the first job interview he'd been able to get in years. He knew he wouldn't be hired if he was late. "It might have been a nice job," he thought, as he picked Lucy up and carried her in his arms all the way to the hospital.

People all around you need help. They might not be bruised and bleeding on the side of the road, but they are broken and hurting inside. It's easy to pass them by. Somebody else will help them, you might think. After all, what can I do? And life gets so busy, it doesn't seem like we have time to get involved.

But Proverbs tells us it's not OK to say, "Not my problem." If you have the power to help people around you, God expects you to help them. It's your job, not somebody else's. Proverbs also says not to put it off. If you can help someone today, don't put it off until tomorrow.

The Bible teaches an awesome truth about those who go out of their way to help others: They're actually helping God himself! When we stand before God, he'll say, "I tell you the truth, whatever you did for one of the least of these brothers of mine, you did for me" (Matthew 25:40).

discussion starters

1. Whom have you encountered who might need your help today? What will you do about it?
2. Why is it important to help today instead of waiting until tomorrow?

Look around you today for people who need your help and **ask** God what he wants you to do for them.

Do not plot harm against your neighbor, who lives trustfully near you. Do not accuse a man for no reason—when he has done you no harm.
—Proverbs 3:29–30

13. wrong is never right

It was January 6, 1994, and one of the world's best female ice skaters and heavily favored gold medalist had just finished preparing and practicing for the Winter Olympics. When Nancy Kerrigan woke up that morning, she never imagined the events that would unravel in just a couple of hours. As she was leaving the ice rink after a practice run, she was hit across the knee with a blunt object by an unidentified man, and she dropped to the ground.

It was later discovered that one of Kerrigan's U.S. ice-skating teammates was behind the attack. Tonya Harding was unable to beat Kerrigan on the ice, so she decided to do exactly what Proverbs 3:29–30 tells us not to do—she devised harm against her neighbor and teammate! She contended with her even when Kerrigan had done her absolutely no harm.

Nearly six months after the attack on Nancy Kerrigan, the U.S. Figure Skating Association stripped Tonya Harding of her 1994 national championship and banned her from the organization for life.

ATTENTION Dare Yourself

When someone else excels in a sport, we can find ourselves wanting to be better than that person. We become frustrated as we sit on the bench and watch from the sidelines as he or she basks in the spotlight. Like Tonya Harding we sometimes feel we have worked just as hard and deserve just as much of the spotlight, and when we don't receive it, we begin to think harmful thoughts against an individual who wishes us no harm.

Nancy Kerrigan was still able to compete in the Olympics that winter, winning the silver medal—missing the gold by the narrowest of margins in Olympic history. As for Harding, her attempt to eliminate her competition by inflicting harm has left her banned for life from something she loves.

discussion starters

1. Do you ever find yourself wishing harm to someone you are in competition with?
2. How do you think you would feel if someone devised harm against you?
3. What do you think is the best way to handle competition among friends?

lifeline

Write down two or three of your best talents. **Thank** God for the gifts he's given you, and **ask** him to help you develop them for his glory.

Listen, my sons, to a father's instruction; pay attention and gain understanding. I give you sound learning, so do not forsake my teaching.

—Proverbs 4:1–2

14. missing dad

Maybe you don't have a father on this earth to whom you can listen. Perhaps you don't have a dad to ask life's most difficult questions. Maybe you don't have his shoulder to cry on. Maybe he's not around to mentor you and show the way.

My dad died last summer. I miss him. Man, how I miss my dad! I miss his great talks, but I'll never forget his example. He was good to Mom and wrote her love notes almost every day. He prayed every night. He'd give you the shirt off his back. The guys who worked for the city by going house to house to collect garbage every Monday and Friday morning were always served a cup of hot coffee and a sweet roll by my dad when they came to our house.

I don't have that example anymore, and I miss it. You may never have had an example like that. Either way, we're longing for that example deep in our hearts, aren't we?

In Romans 8:15 Jesus says, essentially, "From now on, call me Daddy!" God is your Father. Better still, he's your Dad. And he calls his teaching to us wisdom.

I need my heavenly Daddy's wisdom more than I need oxygen. And every time I pick up his Word—the Bible—it's almost as if he's sitting by my side.

discussion starters

1. Why does God call his teaching wisdom?
2. What does it mean to you to call God Father?
3. The Bible is God's Word. How has God taught you by example?

lifeline

When you need wisdom in making a hard decision, *go* to your heavenly Daddy. He'll give you what you need.

> *Put away perversity from your mouth; keep corrupt talk far from your lips.*
>
> *—Proverbs 4:24*

15. deceit leads to death

Mike was one of those boys in high school who played every sport, had the looks, and made the grades. If you were an outsider looking in, you would think the young man had it all together—until one night when everything caught up with Mike.

That night he left his house, telling his parents he was going to stay the night at a good buddy's house. So both parents, assuming Mike was telling the truth, willingly let him go. Mike figured that hiding the truth was acceptable, you know—don't ask, don't tell. If his parents didn't ask the right questions, then he wouldn't tell them. He figured he hadn't really lied, telling his mother that he was going to a friend's house but not mentioning that from there he was going to a party. I doubt if the word *deceit* ever entered his head as he led his mother to believe something that was not completely true.

As Mike's parents sat down to watch the nightly news, the top story of the evening was a five-car accident, which left eight teenagers dead. All were believed to have been intoxicated. Although Mike's parents felt badly for these high-school kids, they were not worried about Mike because they knew where he was. Two hours later they received a phone call telling them that Mike was in the hospital on life support. By the time they were able to get to the hospital, Mike had become number nine in this terrible tragedy.

A deceitful mouth not only cost Mike his life but prevented him from spending his last moments on earth with his parents.

discussion starters

1. How does it make you feel when someone deceives you?
2. What do think prevented Mike from telling his parents about the party?
3. In what ways do you find yourself not telling the whole truth?

lifeline

Examine the words you tell your parents and others. *Determine* to speak only the truth.

Let your eyes look straight ahead, fix your gaze directly before you.

—Proverbs 4:25

16. eyes on the prize

"Look out!" you hear just as the flying golf ball embeds itself in your golf cart.

"Watch out below!" The warning reaches your ears right about the time the brick hits you in the head.

"Keep your head up!" comes a split second before you're drilled by the football player who out-weighs you by fifty pounds.

"Watch it—" Your car smashes through the garage door.

"Eye on the ball!" Thud. (That hurt!)

"Look before you leap!" Splash! Thump. Ugh!

The warnings to keep our eyes open and our minds alert have been many. The bruises and scars are painful reminders of the many times we've forgotten to listen.

You're flunking algebra, and the brilliant girl who sits next to you has the correct answer to the impossible test question in plain view.

You're standing in the checkout line; your eyes catch the *Sports Illustrated* swimsuit issue.

The mirror keeps reminding you that your best friend is five pounds thinner than you.

Let's face it—our eyes can be our best friend or our worst enemy. Our eyes protect us. Our eyes get us into trouble.

The apostle Paul knew this. He wrote in Colossians 3:1–2, "Since, then, you have been raised with

Christ, set your hearts on things above, where Christ is seated at the right hand of God. Set your minds on things above, not on earthly things."

God warned Joshua to follow his law and "do not turn from it to the right or to the left" (Joshua 1:7).

In the Sermon on the Mount, Jesus sealed the case for using wisdom about what we see, because it directly relates to choosing our values: "The eye is the lamp of the body. If your eyes are good, your whole body will be full of light. But if your eyes are bad, your whole body will be full of darkness" (Matthew 6:22–23).

discussion starters

1. What makes our eyes so powerful?
2. What does "eyes on the prize" mean to you?
3. Is there anything your eyes keep going back to that distracts you from the prize?

lifeline

Thank the Lord today for your eyes. *Ask* him to help you use them in a way that will bring honor to him and long life to you.

> *The lips of an adulteress drip honey, and her speech is smoother than oil; but in the end she is bitter as gall, sharp as a double-edged sword. Her feet go down to death; her steps lead straight to the grave. She gives no thought to the way of life; her paths are crooked, but she knows it not.*
>
> —Proverbs 5:3–6

17. smooth

Abercrombie and Fitch has smooth ads. *Rolling Stone* has smooth articles. Eminem and Christina Aguilera have smooth music. The box office sells tickets to smooth movies. Commercials for alcohol (and about every other product) have girls in smooth clothes. Aggressive girls have smooth kisses. Sweet talking guys have smooth lines. Smooth feels good. Smooth looks good. Smooth fills your senses, sells products, and gets dates.

But what happens when smooth isn't smooth anymore? What happens when what looked smooth turns around and bites you—steals your innocence, your conscience, your self-image, and your relationship with God?

I know what happens. For thirty years I've seen it on the tear-stained faces of young people who visit my counseling office. When smooth isn't smooth anymore, it hurts. It really, really hurts.

Saying no is rough. Going against the flow is tough. Saving sex for your marriage partner is rough and tough, especially when the smoothness of young love fills your heart.

But like a rock that resists the flow of the rushing stream, our rough edges will become smooth . . .

in time. This natural process of aging and honing turns rough rocks into smooth gems.

Teens who are saying no to the many smooth messages from sexual entertainment will become gems too—gems of God, gems in marriage, and gems for themselves.

discussion starters

1. What smooth messages have you heard lately?
2. What makes sexy so smooth?
3. What is your kind of smooth?

lifeline

Don't be discouraged if the path of resistance seems a little rough. **Think** of it as the polishing God is doing in your life to turn you into a precious gem.

May you rejoice in the wife of your youth. . . . May you ever be captivated by her love.
—Proverbs 5:18–19

18. the new kind of virginity

The title of today's devotion actually came from the cover of one of America's top magazines. On that cover are two teens who are virgins in real life and proud of it. Less than half of America's teens have traded their potentially special honeymoon for a one-night stand or temporary sexual fix—so these two teens represent millions of young people who have a dream that's stronger than their natural bent to give it all away with each passing emotion.

The Bible wasn't written just for the fun of it. But since God invented all the feelings, passions, and emotions of real fun (fun that lasts), following God's design for sex is fun. It's fun to be in love for a lifetime. It's fun to have a honeymoon that lasts (and actually gets better) for fifty years. It's fun not to have a broken heart. It's fun to wake up in the morning and not worry about unwanted pregnancy. It's fun to look in a mirror and be proud of the person you see.

For those of us who've had moments of giving in, either with our eyes or with our bodies, that's precisely why Jesus came to give us a "new virginity." He can restore our purity in his sight. Best of all, he can give us strength to wait, dedicating ourselves—our eyes, our hands, our mouths, our bodies—to the wife or husband of our dreams.

discussion starters

1. Why does God want us to rejoice with the husband or wife of our youth?
2. What is not fun about premarital sex?
3. Why is premarital oral sex and hand sex against God's plan?

lifeline

Make a list of reasons to wait until marriage for the pleasures of sex. *Keep* the list where you'll see it often.

Go to the ant, you sluggard; consider its ways and be wise! It has no commander, no over- seer or ruler, yet it stores its provisions in summer and gathers its food at harvest.

—Proverbs 6:6–8

19. living for the moment

"I thought I loved him, but he never knew the meaning of the word. He said I didn't love him as much as he loved me, so I set out to prove it. I was his—100 percent his. I went to the abortion clinic by myself to do the one thing I was most against. Bobby stuck around just long enough to make sure I got rid of the evidence (our baby), then he took off. Could I have been more naive?"

—Chicago teenager

"My friends told me that getting high would make my problems go away. That wasn't true at all. Although I only did LSD and PCP one time each, I'll never forget how bad I felt. I actually thought I was going to die."

—Kansas City teenager

The letters that have poured into my mailbox through the years have told the same story in thou- sands of different ways:

"Eat, drink, and be merry, for tomorrow we die."

"If it seems OK at the moment, go for it."

"If it feels good, do it."

"Just this once."

One-night stands, temporary pleasure, and living for the moment have taken a huge toll: drug rehabilitation units packed with addicts; abortion clinics overrun with young girls (about 400,000 per year); sexually transmitted diseases (thirty-eight kinds) spreading rampantly through high-school populations; and sad, guilt-ridden, hopeless hearts scattered throughout school hallways across the country.

Tomorrow's joys require sacrifices today. Tomorrow's pleasures come after today's planning. A lifetime of excitement is the result of today's wisdom.

If the ant in today's proverb (with a brain smaller than a pinhead) can put this principle to work, just imagine how good at it you can become!

discussion starters

1. Why do today's pleasures sometimes seem more compelling than a lifetime of fulfillment?

2. What can you learn from the ant?

3. Hebrews 12:2 tells us that Jesus "for the joy set before him endured the cross." What joys are set before you that will help you endure the pressures of life and make wise choices?

lifeline

Ask God to give you patience as you prepare yourself for the future he has planned for you. **Determine** in your heart that, with his help, you'll do nothing to spoil it.

20. two faces

A scoundrel and villain, who goes about with a corrupt mouth, who winks with his eye, signals with his feet and motions with his fingers, who plots evil with deceit in his heart—he always stirs up dissension. Therefore disaster will overtake him in an instant; he will suddenly be destroyed—without remedy.

—Proverbs 6:12–15

There were times during my junior and senior years in high school when I was two-faced. I wore two masks. I tried to please everybody, and I forgot who I was. Around my parents I wanted to be honest and good. But when I left my house, sometimes I'd turn into a different person. I was fighting an inner battle I didn't think I could win.

A guy in my high school (who didn't think much of me) wrote a satirical "senior will" for our prom. Ours was a small school, so each person's bequest was read aloud. What he said about me burned a hole in my heart. "Joe White," the will said, "leaves his two faces to the drama department." My peer was cruel, but he was right. To this day that statement motivates me to integrity.

Girlfriends' and boyfriends' hearts get broken by two-faced people. Parents get wounded by two-faced kids. Friends don't trust two-faced "friends." And two-faced people don't like what they see in the mirror.

Committing yourself to loving and telling the truth and being loyal to yourself, your parents, and most importantly to God, is hard. The high-school culture makes it extra tough. People turn their backs on you when you don't go along. "Everybody's doing it, but I'm not" can cost you your popularity. But you'll respect yourself! You'll be able to live in harmony with God and with your family. And you'll get to take off your masks and leave them permanently with the drama department.

discussion starters

1. Describe an incident in which you were two-faced.
2. Describe the pressure you sometimes feel to live a lie.
3. How can God give you the freedom to walk with integrity?

lifeline

Decide today to be your very best self—the one God created, not one who has to wear a mask.

21. holy hate

*There are six things the L*ORD* hates, seven that are detestable to him: haughty eyes, a lying tongue, hands that shed innocent blood, a heart that devises wicked schemes, feet that are quick to rush into evil, a false witness who pours out lies and a man who stirs up dissension among brothers.*

—Proverbs 6:16–19

I hate it when people hurt kids.

I hate to hear people take God's name in vain.

I hate the devil when he causes kids I care about to fall.

I hate terrorism.

I hate pornography.

I hate that drug lords get rich off of teenagers who are hopelessly addicted and can't say no to the pusher on the street.

John Wesley has been credited with saying, "Give me one hundred men who hate evil and I will change the world."

Jesus got so angry at people who turned the temple of God into a crowded marketplace that he turned over the tables in fury.

We are made in the image of God, and yes, God is love. But there are activities that God hates, and so should we. Hatred brings motivation. Hatred brings passion. It helps us say no with resolve.

Finding out what God hates makes me run like crazy from those things. My core values are written in stone because of the things I know God hates. If God hates it, I need to hate it.

We can't love God and enjoy the things he hates. Maybe that's why Jesus said, "No one can serve two masters. Either he will hate the one and love the other, or he will be devoted to the one and despise the other" (Matthew 6:24).

discussion starters

1. What things do you hate? Is there a difference between hating things and hating people?
2. As you study the list of things God hates, how does that motivate you?

lifeline

Write down the ten things you hate most. **Check** that list against the things God hates and **ask** him to help you adjust your list to be more like his.

Can a man scoop fire into his lap without his clothes being burned? Can a man walk on hot coals without his feet being scorched?

—Proverbs 6:27–28

22. scorching sin

C. S. Lewis's book *The Lion, the Witch, and the Wardrobe* is a story of how four children discover the land of Narnia by entering a wardrobe. One of those children, Edmund, was not with the other three when they first discovered the enchanted land. Instead, he stumbled upon it by himself.

While there, he met the evil White Witch. At first Edmund was afraid to approach her. But he was strangely attracted. When she spoke nicely to him and he tried her addictive sweets, Edmund fell thoroughly under her spell. The witch promised Edmund more treats and princely status if he would bring the other three children to her.

With the candy still in his stomach, Edmund did his best to trick the rest into coming to see the witch. But the others refused, for they knew what she was really like. Still denying the witch's evil and tempted by the promise of more sweets and becoming a prince, Edmund went alone to her home—and discovered what the White Witch was really like. She fed him stale bread and water. She forced him to ride coatless in her sledge through the night during a snowstorm. And when they walked, she had Edmund tied up and whipped as they marched along. It became clearer by the minute that Edmund had been deceived, and now he desperately wanted out.

Does this sound familiar to you? *The Lion, the Witch, and the Wardrobe* is an allegory of the Word of God. Edmund's attraction to the witch and her promises are much like our attraction to Satan's lies and the temptation to sin. Small steps of compromise lead us down a path of destruction that's difficult to escape. And just as Edmund didn't get away with his deception without suffering in slavery, we won't either. Sin is not something to play around with. As Proverbs says, sin is like fire and hot coals. Touching it will always lead to destruction. No matter how harmless and inviting it looks, sin always burns in the end.

discussion starters

1. How have you suffered from sinful choices in the past?
2. Why is sin attractive at first?
3. How can you avoid giving in to the temptation to sin in the future?

lifeline

With a piece of charcoal, **write** Sin=Fire on a note card and **place** it prominently in your room to remind yourself to avoid being burned by Satan's lies. **Ask** God to help you not give in to the temptation to believe them.

23. m&m's

My son, keep my words and store up my commands within you. Keep my commands and you will live; guard my teachings as the apple of your eye. Bind them on your fingers; write them on the tablet of your heart.

—Proverbs 7:1–3

An M&M diet—sounds pretty tasty, huh? But it's more than just a treat; it's crucial to your survival.

One night as I watched a group of brave coal miners rescue nine trapped workers from 240 feet below the earth's surface in a flooded coal mine, my heart was gripped by the intense drama. Those nine people were on the verge of death, lost in total darkness when—after days of dark, frigid starvation—a narrow opening was drilled with pinpoint accuracy, and the miners were lifted from the mine to safety.

Any man or woman without God's Word hidden in his or her heart is like one of those trapped miners. I'm convinced that each year suicides, alcoholism, unwanted pregnancies, drug addictions, eating disorders, self-mutilations, bitter hearts, and an unending list of pain could be averted with a steady diet of M&M's: **M**emorizing & **M**editating on God's Word daily.

My favorite verse to recite when I'm tempted is Psalm 51:10–12: "Create in me a pure heart, O God, and renew a steadfast spirit within me. Do not cast me from your presence or take your Holy Spirit from me. Restore to me the joy of your salvation and grant me a willing spirit, to sustain me."

Start out with one verse per week. Pick your favorite. Think about it every time you've got a gap in your activities.

The ultimate form of the M&M diet is memorizing whole chapters of the Bible and thinking about them all the time. It takes practice, but if you do it, God promises that you "will be like a tree planted by the water that sends out its roots by the stream. It does not fear when heat comes; its leaves are always green. It has no worries in a year of drought and never fails to bear fruit" (Jeremiah 17:8).

discussion starters

1. Why is hiding (storing) and treasuring God's Word in your heart effective in keeping you from getting trapped or lost?
2. What verse or set of verses are you going to memorize first? Do they mean something special to you?

Set a special goal for hiding and treasuring God's Word, and **share** it with a friend for accountability.

With persuasive words she led him astray; she seduced him with her smooth talk. All at once he followed her like an ox going to the slaughter, like a deer stepping into a noose till an arrow pierces his liver, like a bird darting into a snare, little knowing it will cost him his life.

—*Proverbs 7:21–23*

24. how far is too far?

Three unemployed truck drivers eagerly read the classified ad: "Wanted—skilled truck driver to drive a truck filled with TNT through narrow mountain roads." The president of the trucking company interviewed all three men. To each he asked the same question: "When driving a load of TNT, how close can you get to the edge of the road without falling off the cliff?"

The first man boasted of his great skills. "I can get the rear wheels of the truck twelve inches from the edge. Never fell off yet."

The second driver was even more skilled. "I can get one wheel halfway over the edge and not veer off the pavement."

The third driver humbly replied, "TNT is a dangerous load. I'd stay as far from the edge as I could."

Guess who got the job.

Kissing, heavy French-kissing, petting over clothes, petting under clothes, lying together, sexual intercourse—an "automatic transmission" shifts gears seamlessly from one step of sex to the next. That's how God built men and women for pleasure and procreation in marriage. But if you're more interested in going as far as you can than you are in being careful to stay far away from the edge, watch out! It's a dangerous gamble, and the stakes are high.

The first two truck drivers are like many young people who get hurt in a variety of ways by being involved sexually—on a variety of levels.

The third truck driver is like those who wait to walk the wedding aisle and stay faithfully married with no regrets.

discussion starters

1. How do you feel about the "edge of the cliff" and how close you can come?
2. Why is sex like a truck loaded with TNT?
3. How will you apply today's message to your relationships with those of the opposite sex?

lifeline

Plan fun activities you can do with your boyfriend or girlfriend to spend time together yet stay as far from "the edge" as you can.

To fear the LORD is to hate evil; I hate pride and arrogance, evil behavior and perverse speech.

—*Proverbs 8:13*

25. wise man

While on a two-week summer mission trip, the college group Mark traveled with worked day and night on various campuses in the capital city of Taipei, Taiwan. The night before the trip ended, they all decided to go out dancing. They found a dance hall that seemed like it would be a fun place to hang out.

Mark, however, didn't feel comfortable inside the club. While everyone else danced, he sat struggling to understand why he felt uneasy. Other than his group of friends, the only other people in the club were older men.

As Mark watched his friends having fun, he got upset. "I felt left out, but I knew I was leaving *myself* out. I just couldn't put my finger on why I felt so uncomfortable.

"Suddenly I realized that we were surrounded by evil. No one else seemed to notice because they weren't paying attention. They were just having a good time. But I saw the waitresses taking men into a back room, and they would come out a few minutes later and receive money. I realized we were in a gentlemen's club! My discomfort was due to the presence of sin."

Mark approached his group of friends and told them he thought they should leave. He felt self-conscious, but he couldn't allow them to remain in that atmosphere. Despite a lot of grumbling, the students agreed to go back to the hotel.

"I'm not sorry for dragging them out of there," Mark said. "I knew it was a terrible place to be. One guy told me he thought we should stay because we could be good witnesses to the people there by showing them we were having good, clean fun. But I knew we had to leave. Satan had a foothold there, and we were playing in the devil's playground."

It's not easy to stand up and go against the crowd. But we're commanded to hate evil. Be a leader among your peers, both Christian and non-Christian. Stay away from evil and pursue righteousness.

discussion starters

1. Have you ever had to stand against evil among fellow believers?
2. Why is that difficult to do?
3. Why do we need people to stand up and be leaders among the crowd?

lifeline

Allow yourself to be in tune with the Holy Spirit. *Avoid* evil at all costs, and *take* a stand among your peers.

With me are riches and honor, enduring wealth and prosperity. My fruit is better than fine gold; what I yield surpasses choice silver. I walk in the way of righteousness, along the paths of justice, bestowing wealth on those who love me and making their treasuries full.

—Proverbs 8:18–21

26. his treasure, our reward

My grandmother once wore a beautiful diamond set perfectly atop a quarter-inch-wide ornate wedding band my brother had made from fourteen-karat gold. I decided to give it to my incredible girlfriend, Debbie-Jo, as a symbol of my affection and my pledge to spend a lifetime with her. I hid that ring in a Cracker Jack box and took her atop a beautiful Ozark Mountain cliff overlooking Table Rock Lake with the sun half above and half below the horizon, igniting the water with a fiery reflection.

That evening Debbie-Jo's eyes lit up as brightly as the sun-emblazoned lake. Was it me, or was it the diamond? I'm not sure, but I've learned two things about diamonds after being married to the most incredible woman in the world for twenty-eight years and raising two boys of my own. First, girls love diamonds. Second, the purer, clearer, and more sparklingly perfect a diamond is sharply increases its value.

Christians are a lot like diamonds. The purer they are, the better, more valuable, and more rewarded they are.

Show me a pure mind, and I'll show you a mind full of peace. Show me a pure body, and I'll show you an unspoiled marriage. Show me a pure heart, and I'll show you a godly man and a Christlike woman.

Christ can make your heart pure in God's eyes. When you give Jesus your whole heart, your walk in beautiful, diamondlike purity begins.

discussion starters

1. Why is holiness like a diamond to a girl in love?
2. Practically speaking, how does a person walk in purity?
3. How does Jesus' death on the cross make you pure?

lifeline

Look in a mirror (alone) and *repeat* these words: God, you've made me a diamond, and I want to be the best, brightest, purest, most valuable diamond I can be. Lord, I want to walk in righteousness. Help me to do that.

I [wisdom] was the craftsman at his side. I was filled with delight day after day, rejoicing always in his presence, rejoicing in his whole world and delighting in mankind.

—Proverbs 8:30–31

27. tool for life

If you've ever seen a carpenter at work, you understand how much skill is involved in what he or she does. I happen to know the nail-driving champion of the South. This man can drive fifty-one nails in one minute! I've watched him work, and I'm amazed at what he can do with a hammer and a few nails. But he wouldn't be successful without his tools. Before every nail-driving competition, he makes sure he has a hammer in one hand and plenty of nails in the other. Good carpenters know the importance of their tools, and before they begin a project, they lay them all out on the table.

God is the ultimate carpenter. This world and everything in it are the results of his craftsmanship. But even God realizes the importance of tools.

Before he began creating the world, God created wisdom. She became his tool as he laid out heaven and earth. In Proverbs 8:22–23, wisdom tells the story of her creation: "The LORD brought me forth as the first of his works, before his deeds of old; I was appointed from eternity, from the beginning, before the world began."

God has passed on his tool to those of us who are willing to use it. Remember, a carpenter is useless without his hammer. Likewise, God's children are useless without his wisdom.

discussion starters

1. How can you be prepared for the tasks ahead of you each day?
2. What are some ways you can start using wisdom as a tool?

lifeline

Ask the Lord to show you some ways you can be prepared for what lies before you. **Ask** for his guidance as you seek his wisdom.

> *Whoever finds me finds life and receives favor from the LORD. But whoever fails to find me harms himself; all who hate me love death.*
>
> —*Proverbs 8:35–36*

28. finding life

Sin looks like fun! Hollywood paints the picture with bells and whistles, illuminating it with flashy, neon lights and adorning it with romantic music. With airbrushes and makeovers, models receive the Midas touch. Their broken hearts and defrauded dreams are covered up with incredible skill. Box offices rake in millions of dollars while young people are led down the same real-life path as those who painted the jaded picture.

God warns with insight and foresight, "You shall not covet" (Exodus 20:17). Jesus puts it in his typical easy-to-understand, practical style: "You have heard that it was said, 'Do not commit adultery.' But I tell you that anyone who looks at a woman lustfully has already committed adultery with her in his heart" (Matthew 5:27–28).

Beer commercials parade lusty bodies and carefree beach parties across the TV screen. Never do they show ambulances leaving the ensuing drunk-driving accident or the alcoholics' broken homes and broken hearts.

ATTENTION
Dare
Yourself

Drug pushers who roam school hallways boast smorgasbords of meth, crack, coke, and weed. "Smoke out for a great high." "Party on and forget your troubles this weekend." They mask their personal despair. The sickening dry-outs, shallow self-respect, and countless victims of their greed are hidden with a magician's skill.

But the Bible takes us atop Mount Perspective and helps us see through the shallow veneer. Sin satisfies for a season. Then what? Then, sin hurts for life.

discussion starters

1. Why does a person who loves God love life, and why does one who loves sin love death?
2. In practical ways, how do today's Bible verses and devotion address the choices you're having to make?

lifeline

Make it a point today to look around you—really look. Do your friends and classmates seem to be loving life or just enjoying the moment, regardless of the consequences? **Ask** God for wisdom to know the difference in your own life.

The woman Folly is loud; she is undisciplined and without knowledge. She sits at the door of her house, on a seat at the highest point of the city, calling out to those who pass by, who go straight on their way. "Let all who are simple come in here!" she says to those who lack judgment.

—Proverbs 9:13–16

29. look out!

A few years ago, on a beautiful spring evening, my friend Clint and I decided to go jogging. As we proceeded down the running trail that surrounded the university, Clint saw another friend on the sidewalk. We were going at a moderate pace, and Clint didn't want to stop and lose rhythm, so he called out hello as he passed by. He turned his head and waved, still looking back as his friend returned the greeting. I didn't have time to warn him about the pole.

BAM! Clint slammed into a street sign and staggered off the path into the middle of the road. (Fortunately, no cars were coming.) A number of people saw this happen, and I must admit it's one of the funnier things I've witnessed.

Clint quickly regained his composure and kept running as though nothing had happened. His mishap was hard to ignore, though, because for days he modeled a large bruise on the side of his face as a reminder.

Clint had taken his eyes off the course for just a moment, but it was long enough that he didn't see the sign in his path. We're all running along the trail of life. As we jog forward, there will be distractions. Some things will divert our eyes from the path, and that's where danger lurks.

Folly, or sin, is constantly trying to get your attention. But beware. If you take your eyes off the path for too long, you're likely to trip, fall, or slam face first into a problem. Don't answer folly's cry. Keep your eyes on the path wisdom has laid out before you.

discussion starters

1. Have you ever run into a problem that could have been avoided had you only been paying better attention?
2. What are some things that commonly distract you? Identify some sources the enemy uses to try to get you to take your eyes off the path.
3. How can you combat the enemy's attempts at distracting you?

lifeline

Ask the Lord to reveal to you weaknesses that cause you to turn your eyes from the wise path of life.

The LORD does not let the righteous go hungry but he thwarts the craving of the wicked.

—*Proverbs 10:3*

30. are you hungry?

Some people eat a lot, whether or not they're hungry. Consider the participants in Nathan's Famous Hot Dog Eating Contest, held each year at Coney Island, New York. At the 2003 event, more than three thousand fans cheered as contestants stuffed their faces for—well, for a brief moment of notoriety. Ed "Cookie" Jarvis, standing six feet six inches tall and tipping the scales at 450 pounds, downed thirty frankfurters (buns and all) in just twelve minutes. The championship didn't go to him, however, but to Japan's Takeru "Tsunami" Kobayashi. In the first two minutes alone, the five-foot-seven-inch, 145-pound marvel consumed thirteen hot dogs toward his crown-winning grand total of forty-four. That's an average of one hot dog every sixteen seconds!

Truly hungry people, by contrast, need no special motivation to eat. A homeless person was given enough change by a passerby to purchase a loaf of bread. Famished, he tore open the bread wrapper and began stuffing the loaf by handfuls into his mouth. At that moment, satisfying his hunger was more important than anything else in life.

God cares about our physical hunger and graciously provides the food our bodies require. There's another type of hunger—spiritual hunger—that he wants to satisfy as well. Spiritual hunger is the desire to know God, experience his presence, and hear him speak to us through his Word, the Bible. It's a desire to live a pure life and share the good news of Christ's salvation with others. God is willing to give us all we hunger for—but how hungry are we?

Certain things can dull our spiritual appetites if we let them. Take television. Stan was in the habit of switching on the TV the moment he arrived home from school. He would watch it, essentially non-stop, until bedtime six or seven hours later. With the characters and plot lines of his favorite shows continually on his mind, it's not surprising that he spent little time in daily prayer beyond "Now I lay me down to sleep." Other things not harmful in themselves—music, sports, or friends, for example—can also diminish our spiritual hunger if we allow them to preoccupy us. Of course, sin of any kind will take the edge off our desire for God.

Is satisfying your hunger for God more important to you than anything else in life? He will satisfy that hunger if you will reach out to him.

discussion starters

1. Why do you think some Christians are more "into" God than others?
2. What can you do to increase your spiritual appetite?
3. What did Jesus have to say about spiritual hunger? (Hint: Read Matthew 5:6.)

lifeline

Take inventory of the things in your life that affect your hunger for God. **Ask** him to help you cut back on those which are dulling your spiritual appetite.

Hatred stirs up dissension, but love covers over all wrongs.

—*Proverbs 10:12*

31. the only cure for hate

During the month of April 1999, hate would change the lives of an entire nation.

Dylan Klebold and Eric Harris were constantly teased and picked on by other students. They were different from their classmates and were continually laughed at and ridiculed. They were tormented so much that they developed a hatred for their tormentors and were continually filled with strife.

Eventually the hatred building inside of them exploded. On that April morning they killed twelve students at Columbine High School and injured several others. After they finished releasing their hate toward their peers, they turned that same hate they had for life on themselves and committed suicide.

This tragic morning sent the entire country into shock, and many Americans found themselves hating Klebold and Harris for their actions. Isn't it amazing how hate just creates more hate? The good news is that the same rule applies to love! Proverbs 10:12 makes it very clear that hate is destructive. Rather than hating others, we should allow love (Christ) to cover their transgressions; we are to love others as Christ loves them.

discussion starters

1. How does it make you feel when someone says they hate you?
2. What is the only love that can cover your transgressions (sins)?
3. Do you see kids at your school get picked on? What do you do about it?

lifeline

Think about your daily interactions with others. **Determine** to make a big difference by offering small kindnesses throughout your day.

He who heeds discipline shows the way to life, but whoever ignores correction leads others astray.

—Proverbs 10:17

32. heart for discipline

Thirty beautiful, young mimosa trees adorn our newest camp, K-Kaui. Turning a picturesque Ozark Mountain lakefront property into a Polynesian paradise is a bit of a challenge, but the long, lacy leaves and beautiful pink blossoms of the mimosa trees will be one of the many floral additions that bring Hawaii to Missouri.

Today is "prune the mimosas day." The middle of winter is the time to cut the long, young limbs so that next spring many, many more new branches will begin to grow, and the trees will be lush, thick, and breathtaking in beauty.

Discipline is never pleasant. When we are receiving discipline, we hate it. We feel distrusted, mistreated, arrogant, and prideful. But when we realize that God is purposely pruning us through our authorities so that our lives will be fruitful and meaningful, our attitude toward discipline improves, and we can actually appreciate it.

When my son got his first car, he wrote out a contract that we signed. It outlined his pledge to drive within the limits of the law and live a life that is pleasing to God.

One night his foot got real heavy on the accelerator, and he was apprehended by the highway patrol. He called me immediately and assured me that the car keys would be on my desk for the next thirty days, as the contract specified. No arguments, no discussion, case closed. Like me he made other mistakes during high school, but he always received his discipline humbly and participated in it with his heart. He was wise enough to know he needed it.

God has blessed that lad immensely.

discussion starters

1. Why is discipline such an important asset to our growth?
2. How can you change from one who "hates discipline" to one who accepts it as God's pruning tool to make your life fruitful and fulfilling?
3. What discipline—from God or earthly authorities—have you received lately? What did you learn?

lifeline

Choose to see life's discipline as a chance to grow and mature.

The prospect of the righteous is joy, but the hopes of the wicked come to nothing.

—*Proverbs 10:28*

33. is that all there is?

"That's it? That's all there is?" Concertgoers in Mexico City looked at one another in utter disbelief. For months they had anticipated the arrival of the internationally famous pop star. They had gladly endured long lines and paid top-dollar ticket prices for the privilege of hearing their idol in person. But to their dismay, the long-awaited concert ended almost as quickly as it began. After a few songs, concerns over weather conditions prompted the singer to halt the performance. "I'm sorry, Mexico. I love you. Bye," she told the crowd as she exited the stage. That was it. It was over. She hadn't even finished the song she was singing.

The crowd, understandably upset, yelled "Fraud!" and pelted the stage with the singer's paraphernalia. Later they were offered ticket refunds. Even so, ill will toward the singer spread as the story was reported by international media.

"That's it? That's all there is?" Many ask this same question—not about a concert but about life. Without a belief system that provides for life after death, they find that their relatively short existence on earth has little meaning.

Christians have a different outlook. They know that no matter how difficult this life may be, something better is coming. Their prospect is joy—the eternal joy of being in the presence of their heavenly Father.

How do you picture heaven? If you're expecting winged people with bored expressions floating on clouds and playing harps—boy, are you going to be surprised. Heaven will be a blast! Our happiest times on earth won't compare to the joy we'll experience there.

Of course, not everyone will go to heaven. Only the righteous will be allowed into God's presence. But no human being can ever be righteous through his or her own efforts. The righteousness God requires comes only through his Son, Jesus. When we acknowledge his death for our sins and place our trust in him to save us, he makes his perfect righteousness ours. Then we can lay claim to his promise of eternal life with him someday. Now that's a happy ending!

discussion starters

1. Do you think about heaven often? Why or why not?
2. How might God's promise of eternity with him help a Christian who is suffering persecution?
3. Recall some of the things the Bible tells us about heaven. Which do you look forward to the most?

lifeline

When life gets rough, **remind** yourself of the bright future that awaits you in heaven.

Wealth is worthless in the day of wrath, but righteousness delivers from death.

—Proverbs 11:4

34. what do you value?

Listed below are the "Top 5" things you'll *never* hear someone say just before they die.

I wonder what my stock report looks like today.

I hope I get a good interest rate on my bank note.

What's the price of gold this week?

Honey, did you pick up our American Express travelers checks before we left?

Where's my M-A-S-T-E-R C-A-R-D!?!

Watch any honest movie or hear any real life story and *everyone* says the same thing just before they die, "God, please save me." Most atheists turn to God just before a plane crash!

When the great ship *Titanic* sank in 1912, no one cared about who had the biggest bank accounts, the nicest clothes, the hottest car, the most valuable diamonds, or the biggest paycheck. That night when "the greatest ship that ever sailed the sea" began to disappear beneath the icy North Arctic waters, everyone scrambled for a lifeboat!

Wealth and prestige mean nothing to a man on his deathbed. There's no distinction between wealthy and poor in heaven or in hell. On Judgment Day each of us will stand alone before God, and we'll be held accountable for all our deeds. No amount of riches can buy reconciliation with our maker.

It's interesting to note what it is we value when life is smooth and happy and how those values change when we hit rough spots. Let's work to redirect our values so that our "crisis" values flow over to our good days.

discussion starters

1. What in your life do you value the most?
2. If life is approximately seventy to eighty years on earth and if eternity is forever, how can you reflect that value by what you prioritize on earth?

lifeline

Draw a line down the middle of a piece of paper. On the left side, *make a list* of what's important to you when life is easy and going great. On the right side, *list* what was important to you during the most difficult time of your life. *Determine* to move the list on the right into your whole life.

He who goes about as a tale-bearer reveals secrets, but he who is trustworthy conceals a matter.

—Proverbs 11:13 NASB

35. bite your tongue

The United States government has a branch called the Central Intelligence Agency, better known as the CIA. This agency is responsible for conducting top-secret missions of the United States. In order for anyone to become a CIA operative, they must undergo severe testing and training—everything from physical fitness and reaction time to IQ tests. After four weeks of very intensive training, the applicants are unexpectedly tested.

These men and women are captured by those who they believe are the enemy. They are interrogated intensely for days to see if they will reveal the secret of who they are. If they withstand this final test, they officially become a CIA operative. If they reveal their secret, they will never have the opportunity to become an operative. They have proven themselves to be untrustworthy—unable to keep a secret!

Proverbs tells us that a talebearer reveals secrets, but a trustworthy man conceals them. A recruit's grueling weeks of giving it everything he or she had to become a CIA operative are all in vain if that recruit is unable to keep a secret. Just as a tiny spark can set an entire forest aflame, the book of James reminds us, an untrustworthy tongue can spoil an entire friendship or bring intense hurt to a person we love.

discussion starters

1. How do you feel when someone shares a secret with you?
2. Why is it difficult to trust someone who gossips?
3. Who are people you know you can trust? Why?

lifeline

Ask God to help you think before you speak, to put a guard on your mouth.

A kindhearted woman gains respect, but ruthless men gain only wealth. A kind man benefits himself, but a cruel man brings trouble on himself.

—*Proverbs 11:16–17*

36. kindness

Gladys Aylward, a poor, unmarried servant woman, knew God had called her to go as a missionary to China. She was almost prevented from fulfilling her call by the China Inland Mission in England because they considered her unqualified. But Gladys trusted God, and she worked diligently until she had saved enough money to send herself to China.

With the help of her employer, Gladys contacted an elderly missionary woman who agreed to work with her even though Gladys wasn't supported by a missionary organization. When the older missionary died, Gladys continued the work. When the Chinese-Japanese war began, she refused the orders of the Chinese government to return to England for her own safety.

Gladys worked happily among the Chinese people, whom she loved despite their mistrust of her motives. She cared for the sick and wounded and provided food for refugees fleeing the approaching Japanese army. She also saved the lives of many children who had been orphaned by the fighting. When the Japanese army came near her village, Gladys knew she must take the children to another mission station where they would be safe.

With God's help she began a dangerous trek over the mountains in order to avoid the Japanese army. Throughout the journey Gladys continued to take in more orphan children from each village the weary band passed. Gladys never turned away a needy soul, and by God's providence and her kindness, she was able to save the lives of one hundred orphans. The native Chinese people who had originally treated her with mistrust began to love and trust her. The powerful ruling mandarin, or province governor, accepted Christ as his Savior because of Gladys's example.

Gladys Aylward won the respect and trust from a hostile government and a needy, war-torn nation because of her kindness to the orphans, which spoke volumes about her faith—more than her words ever could. Consider how Jesus was known for his kindness to the undeserving and imagine how your kindness can impact those around you. The kindness you show to the needy will earn you the respect of others.

discussion starters

1. Which acts of kindness have made the biggest impact in your life?
2. Relate a time when you were kind to someone without the promise of kindness in return.
3. In the first century, nonbelievers began to call believers in Christ *Christians*—literally, "little Christs." How does kindness make us more like Jesus?

lifeline

Jesus said that if we show kindness to someone who will return the favor, few people will be impressed. But if we're kind to strangers and to the needy, our kindness will be a witness to others. *Make* a plan to show kindness to someone who cannot be kind to you in return.

37. give it away

One man gives freely, yet gains even more; another withholds unduly, but comes to poverty. A generous man will prosper; he who refreshes others will himself be refreshed.

—Proverbs 11:24–25

Is Zell Kravinsky supergenerous—or insane?

What person would spend his life making millions of dollars in order to give it away? And what person would even consider giving one of his kidneys to an impoverished woman after meeting her just one time?

The enjoyment Kravinsky has experienced through giving baffles many people and leaves them feeling uncomfortable. His level of giving is beyond the ordinary, so people conclude that he must be crazy (or the rest of us are selfish).

Kravinsky, unlike most of his critics, has discovered that money is not a treasure but a tool. He has used it to alleviate suffering and to promote the health and well-being of others. He has donated millions of dollars to institutions working in the interest of public health. He knew he could always make more money through real-estate investments—and he would give that away too.

Some of Kravinsky's public comments probably have rattled people. He believes that no one should have two houses when people are homeless, and no one should have two kidneys while others struggle to live without one.

People don't understand his motive, but Kravinsky's actions seem to embody the message of the New Testament prophet John the Baptist: "The man with two tunics should share with him who has none" (Luke 3:11). This goes against the usual practice of heaping up riches for one's own pleasure and comfort.

Those who have benefited from Kravinsky's generosity consider him a hero. But the man admits he doesn't feel like a hero. He believes he can never give enough—never be good enough or fulfill his desire to be totally self-sacrificing. And he's right. No human gift can ever match the gift God gave to the world through the life and death of his Son. Jesus gave himself for all the needs of humanity—once and for all.

His was the perfect sacrifice.

Giving is part of God's nature. He has built the law of sowing and reaping into the universe. He has promised to bless those who give in His name—even if it's just a cup of cold water.

When we give, it isn't to achieve righteousness. Giving is simply an overflowing of the gifts God has freely given to us.

discussion starters

1. Should giving be spontaneous or planned? What are the pros and cons of each approach?
2. What does it mean to "give of yourself"?

lifeline

Consider giving your time and energy to a worthy cause. **Keep** a journal of your experience and the feelings it produced in you and in those you served.

> *A righteous man cares for the needs of his animal, but the kindest acts of the wicked are cruel.*
>
> —Proverbs 12:10

38. to the rescue

The television show *Animal Precinct,* on the Animal Planet channel, can be hard to watch. It's an education for people who aren't aware of how widespread pet abuse is.

But officials in New York City do know—which is why they operate the Humane Law Enforcement Department (HLE), a branch of the American Society for the Prevention of Cruelty to Animals. *Animal Precinct* documents these officers' work. In one episode Annemarie Lucas and JoAnn Sandano, members of the force, responded to a complaint in Brooklyn about three dogs in distress. The officers found all three neglected, tick infested, and near starvation.

As a result of their investigation, the dogs' owner was sentenced to three years' probation and was not permitted to have any contact with animals during that time. The dogs were all adopted—one of them, a golden retriever mix, by Dave Price, a New York City TV weatherman.

"I definitely spoil him," Price reported. "He sleeps on the bed with me, of course. He adores coming on the set with me and loves when he has an audience—he even shakes people's hands. He is also extremely smart! One day at the beach—it was one of those really hot summer days here in New York City—Chance knew to dig deep enough in the sand until it became cool. After he dug his hole he climbed right in to cool off. He's brilliant!"

Another of the dogs was rescued by a suburban family. His new owner, whose name is Ruth, told

Animal Precinct that "he loves everyone he meets and, of course, sleeps in the bed with me. He also loves his toys, especially a doll which he carries around with him. We are so happy that we could give him a better life!"

Thousands of dogs have similar sad stories but without happy endings. They might have been cared for as puppies, but as they got older, their families just stopped taking time for them. Many are chained outdoors every second of their lives, lucky if they get food and water on a given day.

Yet these two new owners know how to treat a pet—as a member of the family.

And treating animals kindly isn't just a good thought—it's also the will of God, who considers it a sign of a righteous person. God made animals, and he knows how much love and companionship they have to give, asking very little in return. What can you offer?

discussion starters

1. Do you have, or have you ever had, a pet? Describe your relationship with that animal.
2. How does it make you feel to treat an animal kindly? How do such acts affect you as a person? What do they say about you as a person?

lifeline

Volunteer at an animal shelter. It's one way to show Christian kindness without even saying a word.

Reckless words pierce like a sword, but the tongue of the wise brings healing.

—Proverbs 12:18

39. throw me the ball!

Words hurt.

No, they really do.

Being a teenager in today's world, you probably already know this. Sometimes people can be cruel with the words they use. But scientists have recently uncovered evidence that feelings hurt in the same way physical pain does.

According to the American Association for the Advancement of Science, researchers had several young test subjects play a video game that depicts three players tossing around a ball. The computer controlled two of the players, but the subjects were told that actual people in another room were controlling them.

At first the subjects were allowed to participate with the other two "players." But then the two computer players started throwing the ball only to each other, ignoring the human players.

Scientists studied the players' brain scans throughout the process. When the test subjects were not allowed to play with the two computer players because of what the scientists called "technical difficulties," there wasn't much reaction in the brain—besides mild boredom perhaps. But later when the subjects thought the two other players were deliberately excluding them, a certain area of the brain was activated—the same area that processes physical pain.

In short, the hurt you feel from being punched or from being excluded and teased are one and the same, as far as your brain is concerned.

If that study—and your own experiences—aren't enough to convince you that words hurt, check out today's Scripture passage. Many centuries ago God didn't need a science experiment to understand those hurt feelings. He knows exactly how it feels.

You probably don't need an experiment either. But it's an interesting study nonetheless, and perhaps a reminder that your feelings aren't the only ones that are vulnerable to teasing and exclusion. When you act that way toward other people, they have the same pain reaction. It's human nature.

It's the Lord's will that no one go through that kind of pain, and as Christians we need to be extra careful that we don't say or do anything that would hurt a friend, family member, or acquaintance. Instead, we should build up someone's feelings with words that heal.

In the end, feelings are much more than a game.

discussion starters

1. How do you feel when you're deliberately left out or made fun of? Have you ever treated others that way?
2. How can the words you use bring healing and   iness to others? How can your Christian testimony be strengthened by such words?

lifeline

Think about your friends and acquaintances at school or church. Who among them could use a kind word this week? **Make** a point of complimenting those people, letting them know how much they mean to you or how much you admire them in some way.

An anxious heart weighs a man down, but a kind word cheers him up.

—*Proverbs 12:25*

40. get your game on

Growing up, basketball was not only a part of Lee's life—it was his life. He loved the game and could almost always be found out on the court. In fact, as a child he was known to sleep with his basketball.

Lee's dream to play in college came true when he received a full basketball scholarship. He had finally made it. But Lee had one problem. He suffered from pregame jitters. Anyone who plays sports, especially at that level, knows the anxiety that hits before a game. There were times Lee was so worried that he became physically ill. His driving desire to excel and the intensity of the moment would consume him, and he felt almost paralyzed.

Fortunately, Lee was blessed with an older brother who always encouraged him and calmed his nerves. Eric would take Lee aside before a game and get him focused on his strengths.

Using simple phrases like "You're shooting the ball great lately; keep it up," "The guy covering you can't stop you tonight," and "Play like you're in the backyard with all the guys," Eric gave Lee the freedom to go out and play with confidence.

Worry can gnaw at us until we're little more than a pool of nerves.

Anxiety tends to paralyze us, keeping us from moving forward and excelling. But sometimes all it takes to get us going again is a kind word of encouragement. Do you have someone in your life who encourages you? Are you an encouragement to others when they're worried? Don't allow yourself to become weighed down by worry or fear. Find someone who will encourage you and lift you up when you need a boost.

discussion starters

1. What are some things that cause you to be anxious or to worry?
2. What can you do to surrender those worries and stresses to the Lord?

lifeline

Determine to help ease someone's fear and anxiety through your kind and encouraging words today.

The sluggard craves and gets nothing, but the desires of the diligent are fully satisfied.

—*Proverbs 13:4*

4.1. wasted talent

Tom was a gifted musician. He could play the piano beautifully, and he had a voice that made your heart skip a beat. He had a good command of the trumpet, trombone, guitar, and hammer dulcimer. But his skills didn't stop there. He was a deep thinker, and he wrote some wonderfully profound lyrics. His talent was phenomenal!

Tom often talked about his desire to be famous, and he hoped to make it big in the recording industry someday. But he was waiting for fame to find him; he never put forth the effort to make his dream come true. As time passed he began making excuses for himself, saying a musician's life isn't practical; he didn't want to have to deal with producers and studios. But really he was just too lazy to get out there and try. Eventually, he stopped writing songs altogether. Now, years later, Tom has found no more success than he did when we were in high school.

It's a pity to see such talent wasted. Would he have made it big in the recording industry? Who knows? Certainly not Tom. He'll never find out, and that's what causes him the greatest discontent these days. He gave up on his dream before he gave it a chance to come true.

Take some time to figure out what your talents and gifts are. In light of those talents, what would you like to do in life? Dream for a moment. How could you most glorify God with the talents he's given you?

To accomplish your dreams, all you need is a little talent, a lot of faith, dependence on the Lord, and diligence. This is a prescription for success. Are you up to the challenge?

discussion starters

1. What are some of the gifts God has blessed you with? (Talent is not only manifested in performing. People skills, encouragement, compassion, enthusiasm—these and many others are gifts and talents.)
2. How can you best glorify God using those gifts?
3. What are your dreams?

lifeline

Take a moment to write out some short- and long-term goals. How are your short-term goals helping you attain your long-term dreams?

Dishonest money dwindles away, but he who gathers money little by little makes it grow.

—*Proverbs 13:11*

42. easy come, easy go

King Solomon, the author of this proverb, has been called the wisest man in the world. Under his leadership Israel had a golden age. Peace and prosperity lured rulers from hundreds of miles around to find out Solomon's secret and see for themselves the city where "the king made silver as common . . . as stones" (1 Kings 10:27). Visitors went away impressed and probably loaded down with exotic gifts.

What do you get for a person who has everything? How about a little discipline? Despite every possible advantage, Solomon didn't live by his own good advice.

Easy come, easy go. Only the best of everything would do for Solomon. Incredibly, even his wealth couldn't equal his excess. He had to establish a system to tax Israel's people to cover the costs of his own decadent desires. He conscripted workers and then mistreated them. He even gave away some cities in his kingdom to another king. The good life was ending, and Solomon didn't have anything to fall back on.

He had ignored his own wisdom and turned his back on God.

The Bible doesn't condemn wealth, whether little or much. But the Bible has a lot to say about how wealth is gained and how it is used. Luke tells a true story about a tax collector named Zacchaeus. Tax collectors were considered criminals, and many were. They often overcharged the people and kept the extra for themselves. When Jesus accepted an invitation to visit this man's house and share a meal with him, people couldn't believe that this holy teacher would be seen in a tax-collector's home. But meeting Jesus instantly changed Zacchaeus's priorities: "Here and now I give half of my possessions to the poor, and if I have cheated anybody out of anything, I will pay back four times the amount" (Luke 19:8).

A famous ancient philosopher named Epicurus said, "Wealth consists not in having great possessions but in having few wants."

Another famous teacher pointed to the lilies growing wild in the field and made a startling comparison: "Not even Solomon in all his splendor was dressed like one of these" (Matthew 6:29).

Solomon wasn't smart enough to follow his own advice, but you can be. The splendor of a disciplined life and a clear conscience outlasts treasuries full of gold.

discussion starters

1. Consider this equation: If you save ten dollars a month from age fifteen to age seventy, and if the money earns an average of just 5 percent a year, you will enjoy a total of $34,362. Maybe that doesn't sound like much, but you will have actually contributed only $6,600! The remainder is interest earned. Would you miss $2.50 a week if you started saving now?

2. What are some other ways you can be wise about your money?

lifeline

Satan is working hard to tempt you with glitter and gloss. **Ask** God to give you wisdom to discern the difference between fool's gold and real treasure.

Poverty and shame will come to him who neglects discipline. But he who regards reproof will be honored.

—Proverbs 13:18 NASB

43. pushing the rock

There's a story of a man who was asleep one night in his cabin when suddenly his room was filled with light and the Lord appeared. The Lord told the man he had a work for him to do and showed him a large rock in front of his cabin. The Lord explained that the man was to push against the rock with all his might.

This the man did—day after day. For many years he toiled from sun up to sun down, his shoulders set squarely against the cold, massive surface of the unmoving rock, pushing with all his might. Each night the man returned to his cabin, sore and completely worn out, feeling that his entire day had been spent in vain.

Seeing that the man was showing signs of discouragement, Satan decided to enter the picture, placing thoughts into the man's mind: "You have been pushing against that rock for a long time, and it hasn't budged an inch! Why kill yourself over this? You are never going to move it!" Thus the devil did all he could to convince the man that the task was impossible and that he was a failure.

Discouraged and disheartened, the man became convinced. "Why am I killing myself over this?" he thought. "I'll just put in my time, giving the minimum of effort, that will be good enough." Fortunately, before he gave in to the devil, the man decided to make it a matter of prayer and take his troubled thoughts to the Lord.

"Lord," he said, "I have labored long and hard in your service, putting all my strength to do that which you have asked. Yet, after all this time, I have not even budged that rock a half a millimeter. What is wrong? Why am I failing?"

To this the Lord responded compassionately. "My friend, when long ago I asked you to serve me and accept this discipline, I told you that your task was to push against the rock with all your strength. This you have done. Never once did I tell you that I expected you to move it. Your task was to push. Now you come to me, your strength spent, thinking that you have failed."

The Lord continued, "But is that really so? Look at yourself. Your arms are strong and muscled, your back broad, your hands callused from constant pressure, and your legs have become massive and hard. Through opposition you have grown much and your abilities now surpass anything you had before. No, you haven't moved the rock, but you have been obedient and disciplined. Now, my friend, I will move the rock!"

discussion starters

1. In what areas are you discouraged with God?
2. In what areas are you disciplined?
3. Have you ever neglected discipline from a parent, a coach, or even God? What lesson did you miss out on?

lifeline

Ask God to give you a new vision of the difficulties in your life. *Thank* him for the maturity they bring.

He who walks with the wise grows wise, but
a companion of fools suffers harm.

—Proverbs 13:20

44. walk wisely

Meagan's mom died when she was a child, and six years after that, she lost her father as well. Being the oldest of three children, Meagan felt the need to take care of her siblings. But the stress proved too much for her, and she soon found solace with the wrong crowd.

Meagan had a godly extended family, and they warned her numerous times about the danger of being involved with the people she called her friends. But Meagan would not be deterred, and she headed down a long, painful path for many years. It was a path that started out as many forms of self-destruction do: peer pressure.

Although Meagan is now a happy, healthy young woman working her way through college, it took her a long time to finally be able to say she feels good about where and who she is.

"I thought the people I was hanging out with would make me happy," she said. "But they were just using me. I was just so angry, and I wanted so badly to make my own choices. But instead of separating myself from the crowd, I became one of them. Drugs and alcohol were part of the package."

Meagan still has to work hard to overcome the evil that penetrated her life during those dark years. But she has come to understand that who you spend your time with really does matter. She stays away from places and people who would bring her down.

"It's a temptation," she said. "If I step into a bar, I'll struggle with desire for a drink all night. If I'm around someone who does drugs, I will literally fight a mental battle not to join them. So, to avoid all that struggle, I simply avoid those people and situations."

That's the wisdom of experience, my friends. Meagan will forever bear scars from her years of partying. But thanks to God's grace, she finally came to a point where she could truly become an individual. She is a woman of grace, and that's due in large part to the fact that she's surrounding herself with godly men and women.

Be careful who you spend your time with. Don't open doors that will be difficult to close.

discussion starters

1. How does peer pressure affect you? Are you easily swayed?
2. With what kind of people have you chosen to surround yourself?
3. Are they having a positive or negative impact on your life? How are you impacting their lives?

lifeline

Make a list of your closest friends and how they affect your life. **Pray** over that list and **ask** the Lord to show you if there are any people or situations you need to distance yourself from.

A good man leaves an inheritance for his children's children, but a sinner's wealth is stored up for the righteous.

—Proverbs 13:22

45. a lasting gift

Jim Cooper didn't grow up learning about God. He came from a broken home during a time when divorce was frowned upon. When he entered the military as a young man and headed off to boot camp, he knew nothing about living a Spirit-led life.

After the war Jim met Betty, and they married. Betty had a similar upbringing, so neither of them felt much need for a spiritual walk with God. But after their second child was born, Jim and Betty met a young preacher who shared the Gospel with them. They realized they were missing God in their lives, and they both accepted the Lord.

After some time of spiritual growth and discipleship, Jim and Betty felt a calling to serve God through foreign missions. They wanted to spread his Word to the ends of the earth. So when the opportunity came to go to South Caicos, a tiny island in the Caribbean, Jim and Betty readily accepted. They packed up their four children and headed south.

Reverend Jim Cooper spent the rest of his life serving the Lord in the Caribbean. He had little material wealth, but he loved people. He founded a number of churches in the Bahamas and a school in Nassau. He served the Lord until the day he died of leukemia when he was only forty-four.

Jim couldn't leave behind a large inheritance, but his and Betty's legacy was what they gave to their children. They started a tradition of love and

dependence on God. While their extended families struggled with numerous heartaches and trials, Jim and Betty held to their strong belief in the almighty God. Today their children—and their thirteen grandchildren—all have made professions of faith in the Lord Jesus Christ.

What Jim and Betty passed on to their children is far more valuable than money. They gave a spiritual inheritance that will last forever.

discussion starters

1. Where does your legacy of belief come from? Does it begin with grandparents or parents?
2. Perhaps you're the first in your family to make a profession of faith in God. How are you going to build up a spiritual inheritance that will forever bless your children's children?
3. When your time has come and you pass from this world into heaven, what would you like people to say about you?

lifeline

Ask God to help you be faithful to him and to leave a spiritual legacy for those you love.

Each heart knows its own bitterness, and no one else can share its joy.

—Proverbs 14:10

46. your heart's joy

In 1994 a team of students left for Minsk, Belarus, for a two-week long mission trip. Ranging in age from fourteen to eighteen, the group had only a vague sense of what to expect as they headed to the former Soviet Union. They had all been through months of training on how to share their faith and testimony with people of another language. They were as prepared as they could be.

When they arrived in Minsk, they were met by a group of Byelorussian students who were thrilled to have American visitors. For the next two weeks, the Americans visited schools, held meetings, and witnessed to the Byelorussians. They saw God work in mighty ways as students committed their lives to him. The Americans were treated like royalty almost everywhere they went, which was both strange and exciting for them.

One highlight of the trip was a visit to an orphanage for handicapped children. The American team was astounded to see the conditions the children lived in, and they spent an entire day encouraging and sharing the gospel with them.

By the time the team left for home, they had all been impacted and changed in some way. They couldn't wait to tell their stories to their families and friends. But when they got home, they found that the people they told didn't seem as interested or excited as the students. They almost seemed bored with the details. No one understood what they had felt and what the experience meant to them.

At a debriefing a week after their return, the students talked with their leader about this. "Don't be so hard on them," he told his frustrated team. "Your families and friends weren't there; they didn't experience the joy and heartache you did. They can't understand."

Your memories and experiences are unique to you. No one else can truly experience your heartache or your sorrow in the same way or as intensely as you do. No one, that is, except the Lord. Pour your heart out and share your joys and sorrows with him. He truly understands and cares.

discussion starters

1. Why is it difficult for us to fully convey our feelings of bitterness and joy?
2. Is your heart filled with bitterness or joy? If so, express it to God. He will listen.

lifeline

Praise the all-knowing Lord for his power. **Ask** him to search your heart and heal your anger or pain. Then **allow** him to rejoice with you.

> *All hard work brings a profit, but mere talk leads only to poverty.*
>
> —Proverbs 14:23

47. go for the gold

Before competing in the Olympics, every athlete must first qualify for his country's Olympic team. These qualification trials are intense and exciting as men and women of all ages strive toward lifelong goals. Many have dedicated years of time, effort, and self-sacrifice to their sport. For a chance to represent their country in this worldwide competition, they'll work through pain, sweat, disappointment, and tears.

During the 2000 gymnastics trials in Boston, I watched several young men and women in amazement as they pushed aside their pain to fight for one of the six coveted spots on the Olympic team. Shannon Miller competed with a stress fracture in her leg; Kristen Maloney had undergone surgery only months before that left her with a metal rod in her leg; Chris Young had torn his Achilles tendon just eight months earlier. They had worked a lifetime to get to that point, and they were willing to work through the pain and discomfort to achieve their goals and be the best in their sport. They were keenly aware of the reward for their hard work—a chance to represent their country at the Olympics and

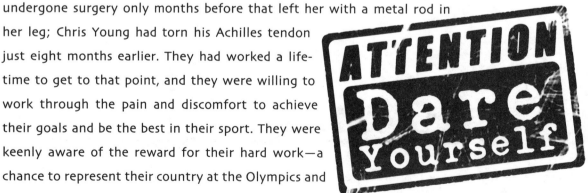

the satisfaction of knowing they're among the world's elite athletes—and they weren't willing to do anything that might risk that opportunity.

Being number one isn't easy. The world's top athletes don't talk their way to the top. Michael Jordan wasn't the greatest basketball player because of his words—he was the greatest because he worked. This is true for anything in life. Top doctors and scientists don't talk their way into a hospital or laboratory; they work.

Working isn't always fun; sometimes it may be boring or even painful. But the most fulfilling accomplishments come through hard work. Dedicate yourself to worthy goals you're passionate about. Be ready to work hard. Do what it takes to be the best you can be.

discussion starters

1. What are some goals you have set for yourself? What are some goals you'd like to set? (Make them realistic.)
2. What do you need to do to accomplish these goals?

lifeline

Ask the Lord to give you the strength and determination to work toward your goals.

The fear of the LORD is a fountain of life, turning a man from the snares of death.

—Proverbs 14:27

48. it's electric

Have you ever felt true fear—the kind that makes you acutely aware of all your senses? I've been scared many times. I've felt my heartbeat quicken as my imagination convinces me of unseen danger. But that doesn't measure up to true, jolting fear.

As I drove home well past midnight recently, the road seemed deserted. I was worn out and just wanted to be in bed. I didn't see the motorcycle rushing up behind me until it roared by, just inches from my window. My heart skipped a beat as I swerved and skidded onto the shoulder of the road.

The motorcycle had disappeared as suddenly as it had appeared. As I slowed to a stop on the side of the road, I felt my fingers tingling and heard a slight ringing in my ears. I felt as though a bolt of electricity had coursed through my body, heightening all of my senses. It was the most intense feeling I've ever experienced.

As I regained my composure, I thought of the Lord's command that we fear him. But I instantly realized that the kind of fear he asks us to have of him is not the kind I felt shivering on the side of the road. He is not some evil to be feared nor is he an unexpected fright in the dark. His power is not like that of the motorcycle that threatened to harm me. His power is loving and kind and full of compassion.

God does not whiz by us on the road of life; he does not leave us alone. Rather, he rides with us as we travel through life, and he'll even take the steering wheel if we'll let him.

As you come before God's throne in prayer, be aware of his power and strength, but do not cower in fear. To fear the Lord is not to be afraid of him—it's to know his almighty power, to respect him, and to be aware of his presence in your life.

discussion starters

1. Have you ever experienced a moment of fear like the one described above?
2. How do you think fearing the Lord can bring life?

lifeline

Ask the Lord to give you a healthy fear of him. **Let** the realization of his power course through your body and bask in the warmth of his love.

He who is slow to anger has great understanding, but he who is quick-tempered exalts folly.

—*Proverbs 14:29* NASB

49. slow to anger

Playing in and coaching Division 1 college football as a defensive lineman didn't exactly give me a passive personality. Every time the center would snap the ball to the quarterback, I was in the middle of a major gang war! If I didn't move quickly and take the fight to the offensive lineman who was trying to demolish me, I would get run over by a stampede of wild horses. I learned to fight and to fight hard.

That was *on* the football field!

Off the football field was a different story.

Last year I spoke at a college event at the University of Colorado where I built a 14-foot cross in front of several hundred college students and shared with them God's amazing gift of love and grace. Hundreds responded to the invitation and gave their hearts to Christ. But one student was outraged! As I leaned against the side wall of the theater, listening to the band play praise and worship music, he approached me in a fury. He got in my face and called me every dirty word ever written on a bathroom wall!

Yeah, I probably could have taken him to the floor.

Yeah, he probably deserved it.

Yeah, something inside of me would have enjoyed making him eat his words.

Yeah, once upon a time, years ago, I probably would have taken issue with him. But when I left football and grew up a little, I left it all on the field. Jesus said, "Love your enemies and pray for them." Jesus said, "Be slow to anger." Jesus said, "Be patient with people." Jesus said, "Vengeance belongs to God."

As the student stormed out of the theater, I prayed for him and still pray for him today, that some-day our paths will cross again—hopefully in heaven where his anger will be calmed forever.

discussion starters

1. Name three people who "provoke you to anger." Compare how you want to react with how you really react. Compare your reaction to the way God wants you to react.
2. In reality, why is God's way best? Why is it best to be "slow to anger"?
3. What does today's verse mean when it says those who are slow to anger have "great understanding"? What do they understand?

lifeline

Ask God to give you the understanding needed to keep your anger in check.

A gentle answer turns away wrath, but a harsh word stirs up anger.

—*Proverbs 15:1*

50. a gentle tongue

When Gideon headed into battle, he took with him only one hundred men—a meager group compared with the vast army of the Midianites they were up against. But God was in control, and he caused the Midianites to turn against one another. Gideon's army simply sat back and watched as their enemy defeated themselves. Not one of the one hundred men had to draw their sword.

As the remainder of the Midianite army fled, Gideon called warriors from the Israelite tribe of Ephraim for help in finishing the job. They cut off the Midianites' escape route, and Israel defeated its enemy.

But after the fighting stopped, the Ephraimites came to Gideon and angrily demanded to know why they had not been called in the first place to help in the battle. "'Why have you treated us like this?'" they whined. "And they criticized him sharply" (Judges 8:1).

It would have been easy for Gideon to respond harshly to their criticism. When we feel attacked or criticized, it's human nature to feel defensive and lash back at those who make us feel that way.

But responding harshly to strong words is a sure way to escalate a conflict. Instead of adding fuel to the fire, Gideon chose to douse the flame with soothing, soft words: "'What have I accomplished compared to you? Aren't the gleanings of Ephraim's grapes better than the full grape harvest of Abiezer? God gave Oreb and Zeeb, the Midianite leaders, into your hands. What was I able to do compared to you?' At this, their resentment against him subsided" (Judges 8:2–3).

Maybe people skills came naturally to Gideon. Perhaps he knew the only way to calm the Ephraimites' anger was to give them credit for the positive things their participation had accomplished.

Gideon wasn't buttering them up or even weaseling his way out of a tight spot; he was merely being a good leader by acknowledging their frustration and their contribution to his success and dealing with their complaints. He took the focus off of what he had accomplished without their help and showed them that he valued and appreciated them.

A kind response is much more effective than a harsh one. Next time you're tempted to let loose verbally and really give someone a piece of your mind, hold your tongue. Speak gently and with kindness instead. Make it your goal to soothe the conflict instead of inflaming it by defending yourself or retaliating. You just might gain (or keep) a friend!

discussion starters

1. How do you deal with people who speak to you harshly?
2. Based on today's proverb, how can you improve your reaction?
3. What steps will you take to make those improvements?

lifeline

Watch for ways you can deal kindly with others. **Bless** those around you with kind words of encouragement.

51. my father's eyes

The devastation caused by a few men on September 11, 2001, was massive. Vicious hatred manifested itself with catastrophic results.

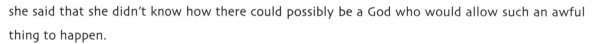

One interview from that tragic morning was particularly heartrending. A reporter spoke with a young woman on the streets of New York City. She looked up at the flaming towers where her husband had worked, unsure whether he was alive or dead. With tears streaming down her face, she said that she didn't know how there could possibly be a God who would allow such an awful thing to happen.

It's difficult to understand how the events of September 11 could have come to pass. That young woman wasn't the only person to question God that day or in the days following. "Where was he?" many inquired.

The answer to that question is simple: He was where he always is—seated on his throne above the heavens, keeping watch over his flock. September 11 was not an oversight. God wasn't caught off guard. The Father's eyes were on his children, and he grieved with them.

Why did it happen? There are no good or right answers. God's ways are mysterious. But even in the midst of mystery, his awesome glory is evident. The book of Job addresses the question of why bad things happen to good people. Though no simple answer is given, we do see that God is constantly working things for the good of those who love him. Satan has no chance for ultimate victory in this world. God has already won the fight, leaving the devil doomed.

What good came out of September 11? Well, for starters, God's name has been mentioned more often on television. All over the world, people cried out to him for strength, peace, and mercy. He has been magnified and glorified despite the attempts of the enemy. America has pulled together, and the Lord has raised up godly men and women to lead our country against the most ominous threat we've ever faced.

discussion starters

1. Have you praised God lately for his mighty provision and comfort?
2. How much do you pray for those who suffered loss during attacks on our country or in military service? If everyone prayed like you, would our nation be in better or worse shape?
3. In the midst of tragedy, do you find yourself questioning God or crying out to him for help and mercy?

lifeline

Say a prayer for our leaders and for those who serve in the armed forces. **Thank** the Lord for their service.

Better a little with the fear of the LORD than great wealth with turmoil.

—Proverbs 15:16

52. when little is much

What would you do if you had a million dollars?

The popularity of lottery games and reality shows proves that millions of people hope to fulfill their fantasy answer. Winning or having wealth can make life easier, but there's something even better than an easy life. Just ask Crystal.

Crystal was born into a poor family that lived in the projects in a large city. Her parents were divorced, and Crystal's mother had to support the family on her own. To make matters even worse, Crystal and her twin sister contracted an illness as toddlers that left them both deaf.

The projects were dirty, dark, smelly, and unsafe. Gangs fought over territories to distribute drugs; crimes frequently brought the city's police, but the gangs held the police at bay with greater firepower.

This was where Crystal grew up.

One day a friend came to the door and invited Crystal to church. She was embarrassed. She didn't have nice clothes to wear, and her life was a mess. She didn't want to be in God's presence until she cleaned up her act.

But her friend persisted, and Crystal went to church. At that one service, Crystal was transformed. She went home to the projects a changed person. God cleaned up her soul.

Now a young mother with children of her own, Crystal worshiped God as she washed dishes and praised him as she tried to make her little apartment a home for her boys. She dusted off her Bible and was thrilled to discover that God's Spirit helped her understand what she read. She prayed constantly for the safety of her sons. And she pleaded with God to intervene in the dark world of the projects.

Crystal didn't win the lottery, and she still lives in project housing. If she weren't deaf, she would hear the gunshots that are not unusual in her neighborhood. She has little material wealth, yet people are drawn to the abundance of joy and contentment Crystal sustains. She tells them about a prize that is better than a million dollars—the treasure of God's love.

There will always be people who seem to have an easier life than you. Maybe you know wealthy families or even someone who won the lottery. But the inner peace and joy that flow out of a relationship with God far surpass external wealth.

discussion starters

1. If someone offered Crystal a million dollars, do you think she would accept? How might her decision, whether yes or no, change her life?
2. Wealth, or even a little extra money, can make life easier. Is this proverb saying that no one should have money?

lifeline

Identify a person you think has it good; then **ask** that person about his or her life. **Be prepared** to share your spiritual wealth.

He who ignores discipline despises himself, but whoever heeds correction gains understanding. The fear of the LORD teaches a man wisdom, and humility comes before honor.

—Proverbs 15:32–33

53. the price of pride

The story is told of a frog who wanted to travel over the top of a tall mountain from a pond he'd grown up in and learned to hate to a beautiful lake on the other side of the peak.

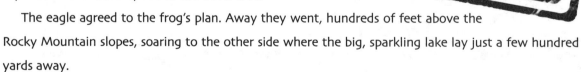

One day as the frog watched an eagle soar high above the clouds, the frog had a brilliant idea. "If I could just get that eagle to hold a piece of string in his talons, I can hold the other end of the string in my mouth. He could fly me to the other side."

The eagle agreed to the frog's plan. Away they went, hundreds of feet above the Rocky Mountain slopes, soaring to the other side where the big, sparkling lake lay just a few hundred yards away.

As the frog hung on to the string by his teeth for the last minute of his ride, he heard someone

below exclaim, "Wow, look at that. What a great idea! I wonder who thought of that?"

The prideful frog couldn't resist the opportunity to brag and opened his mouth to boast, "I diiiiiiid." Splat!

Poor frog. He just couldn't resist telling people how smart he was. Reminds me of myself sometimes, and I want to kick myself for it. How about you? Is pride ever a problem? If so, today's devotion study may be just what the doctor ordered.

discussion starters

1. When you're complimented or commended for something you did well, how does it make you feel?
2. Who really deserves the credit for any good we do here on earth?

lifeline

Next time someone tells you what a great job you did, *give* the glory to God. You'll feel wonderful!

The LORD works out everything for his own ends—even the wicked for a day of disaster.
—Proverbs 16:4

54. the lord's name prevails

No one who saw them will ever forget the images from the Columbine High School shootings. With heavy hearts, people mourned for the students who suffered that day. The names of the shooters—Dylan Klebold and Eric Harris—will continue to incite feelings of anger, pity, fear, and sorrow. As we look at the aftermath of Columbine, however, we can't help but notice how the Lord prevailed.

In the weeks and months after the tragedy, several stories surfaced about students who cried out to God in the midst of the battle—some lost their lives, some didn't, but the Lord's name was called. Suddenly God became the focus on every prime-time news program. People gathered by the thousands to pray together, crying out to God for mercy.

Since then more schools have come under attack by disgruntled students. Even some top authorities agree it's time to look to a higher power for guidance.

Was the Columbine shooting a disaster? Yes. Are all school shootings tragic? Yes. But it's comforting to know that the Lord works—even in the face of great evil—to bring glory to his name and to draw lost and hurting people back to their loving heavenly Father.

God is perfect and incapable of evil. But he can use those who do evil to fulfill his good purposes. God is able to bring beauty from ashes and triumph from tragedy.

discussion starters

1. What are some ways God has received glory from the multiple school shootings in the last few years?
2. What can you do to further the Lord's name and to encourage those who need encouragement?

lifeline

Take some time to thank the Lord for his greatness and his protection. Now *pray* for all of the families who have suffered loss in a school shooting.

Understanding is a fountain of life to those who have it, but folly brings punishment to fools.

—Proverbs 16:22

55. alligator bait

One day as I flipped through the television channels, I came upon a Discovery Channel special on a water hole nestled deep in the jungle. Here species of every kind gathered to cool off, drink, and rest. Hippos, monkeys, deer, and even alligators shared the same serene little pond.

Naturally, with so many different animals in such close quarters, there was bound to be some conflict. Mothers, well aware of potential dangers, kept tight rein over their offspring as they drank and lounged around the refreshing water. Monkey moms held their curious little ones to keep them out of the alligators' reach, and female deer gave warning cries if their fawns wandered too far from their side.

On one particularly hot afternoon, as a group of deer came for a drink, a small fawn timidly inched toward the water's edge. Not comprehending the dangers that lay just beneath the surface, he took a few steps into the refreshing water, ignoring his mother's sounding alarm. Suddenly a spray of water enveloped the startled fawn, and massive jaws clenched onto him. The other deer instinctively sprang back, some turning to run. Only the bewildered mother remained, looking piteously at the spot where her baby had just stood. The fawn never resurfaced.

The naive little deer had not yet gained an understanding of the dangers in his world. Had he listened to his mother's warning, he might have escaped; but his inexperience caused him to wind up as an alligator's lunch.

We all have moments when our inexperience and folly cause us to make mistakes and put us at risk. It's important to listen to the advice and warnings of those who have more wisdom and experience than we do. Although we may not understand at the time, following the advice of those who have our best interests at heart is the wise thing to do. It could even save our lives.

discussion starters

1. Who do you know with life experience who can wisely advise you?
2. Have you received warnings or instruction from someone that you haven't heeded? Why didn't you follow them?
3. What has or might happen as a result?

lifeline

Ask the Lord to bring someone into your life who can teach you understanding and guide you when you need guiding. If you already have someone like that, **thank** the Lord for giving him or her to you.

56. the price of peace

How much money do you have?

How beautiful is she?

How "hot" is he?

What kind of car do you drive?

How fast can he run the forty?

How big is her house?

How skinny is your body?

How muscular is he?

What kind of clothes does she wear?

In our appearance-crazed society, we measure "wealth" in a lot of interesting ways, such as our looks, our athletic ability, our car, our figure, our build.

I've probably met a million kids in my lifetime. I've talked with thousands one-on-one. I've gotten to know hundreds pretty well.

You wanna know what? The most beautiful are usually not the happiest. The most handsome may not be the most fulfilled. The best athlete is not necessarily the most content with himself. The guy with the hottest car is not generally the most peaceful.

In fact looks, talent, and wealth usually have very little to do with a person's inner peace, joy, and sense of fulfillment. In the long run, the things that matter the most aren't the things we can see and possess.

Advertisers unrelentingly work to make us think that *things* are paramount, so they can sell their product.

If people were content with who they are and what they have, clothing and jewelry and diet deals wouldn't sell very well, would they?

Peace—in your family and in yourself—is what really matters. Do you have peace in your life? Inner peace comes from knowing Jesus.

Do you have peace in your family? Peace in your family comes from loving Jesus more than you love yourself.

Do you have joy in your heart? Joy comes from being thankful in all circumstances and serving others more than you serve yourself.

discussion starters

1. Why is inner peace better than beauty?
2. Why is inner joy better than looks?
3. Why is contentment better than riches?

lifeline

Ask God to give you new insight into the value of peace as opposed to appearance and possessions.

The crucible for silver and the furnace for gold, but the LORD tests the heart.

—Proverbs 17:3

57. refiner's fire

One beautiful autumn day, I stumbled upon a fall festival in a nearby park. I decided to check it out, interested primarily in getting a candied apple like the one I'd seen someone else walking out with.

As I was on my sugary search, however, I got sidetracked by the fascinating demonstrations taking place all around me. It was a historic park, so many of the shows revolved around things like blacksmithing, broom making, and other amazing skills.

When I stopped to watch the blacksmith for a while, I was astounded at what this man could do with a piece of metal. He took a long, iron rod and stuck the end of it into a fire. The blue flames engulfed the rod for a few moments before the craftsman pulled it out. It now glowed bright orange.

Then the blacksmith put the rod onto a small metal table and hammered it several times to bend it slightly. He stuck the rod back into the fire to heat it again and molded it some more. Within ten minutes he had made a horseshoe.

I watched him for about thirty minutes as he made everything from nails to spurs, and it started me thinking. We're a lot like that piece of metal—stubborn and unwilling to bend or flex. So God plunges our hardened hearts into the fire of trials. The heat alone seems unbearable, yet we often must learn our lessons by enduring the painful banging of the hammer. We become slightly bent in a new direction.

But God's work isn't done. Like that metal, we also tend to cool quickly and harden, so it's back into the fire. Again God presses and molds us. Slowly we take shape. Not everyone moves at the same pace. Some must spend a little more time in the fire than others.

But one day, when we depart from this earth and enter into the kingdom of God, we will finally be complete and perfect. No longer will we suffer the fire of trials and tribulations, for we will be God's masterpieces.

discussion starters

1. What trials are you experiencing currently?
2. Can you see how God is molding you according to his will?
3. Think about trials you've endured. How have those experiences shaped who you are today?

lifeline

Write down some of the struggles you've experienced. **Thank** God for bringing you through those. **Ask** him to teach you through the trials you're facing today.

The words of a man's mouth are deep waters, but the fountain of wisdom is a bubbling brook.

—Proverbs 18:4

58. it's only words

Amazing, isn't it, that a little breath of air passing from our lungs through a pair of vocal cords over our tongue and shaped into a word through a pair of lips can change a person's life forever!

"Love."

"Hate."

"Revenge."

"Peace."

A man can insincerely say "I love you" to a woman and ruin her life forever, while another man can sincerely say the same three words and bless a woman's life immensely.

The immeasurable power of what we say, like an atomic bomb or atomic energy, can destroy or it can empower with immeasurable magnitude.

Hitler said "kill" and eight million Jews in Germany were slaughtered without mercy.

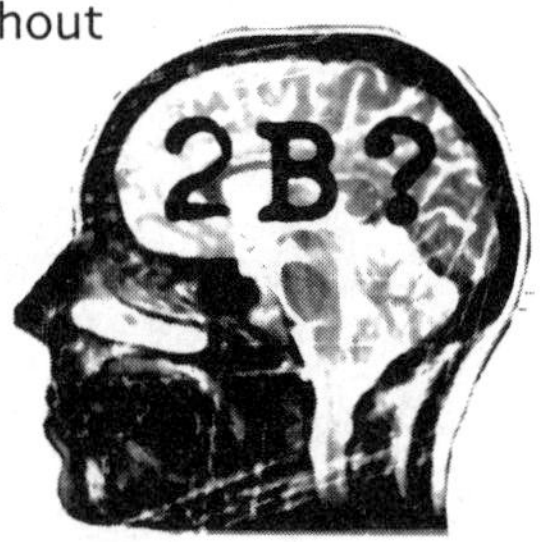

The Supreme Court of the United States said "no" and over forty million unborn American children lost their lives in the following twenty-five years.

An American president said "peace" and the Iron Curtain of Communism fell, and hundreds of millions of people were given the gift of freedom.

Giving and receiving words of wisdom are without a doubt a bubbling brook of life-giving peace, direction, and love. When someone asks you the simple question, "What do you think?" (about a person or an idea), you can destroy or give life by the next words that pass over your lips. You can literally represent Satan or Jesus, depending upon the answer you give.

discussion starters

1. How can you be sure to give "words of wisdom" when asked for your opinion?
2. Discuss the power of words and how this devotional will affect you as you speak to people in your future conversations?
3. Who is the wisest human you know and what makes that person's words so wise?

lifeline

Guard the words of your mouth so that they bubble over with wisdom and bless the lives of all with whom you come into contact.

The name of the LORD is a strong tower; the righteous run to it and are safe.

—*Proverbs 18:10*

59. it's who you know

Have you ever seen the power in a name? The school oddball is safe from taunts and teases if he's befriended by a popular, athletic student. "Don't mess with Nicky," the taunters spread the word. "Justin and his gang will use your face to clean the chalkboards."

Maybe you have an older sister who was successful in school—she was homecoming queen, got straight As, and earned a full scholarship to the best college in the state. Anything you accomplished looked insignificant in comparison. How many teachers have singled you out: "Oh, you have a lot to live up to. Your sister was so smart; I'm sure it runs in the family."

A name does have power—sometimes good, sometimes bad. Consider these "names": Officer, Murderer, Thief, Pastor, Friend, Mother, Liar, Teacher, Father. Depending on the people you know who go by these names, the words alone have power to make you feel safe or scared, happy or nervous, loved or rejected.

The name of Jesus is powerful because Jesus is the Son of the all-powerful God. Teri was fourteen when she experienced the protective power of Jesus' name. Her mother was driving their van on a busy highway. Holiday traffic made the roads more crowded than usual, and Teri's mom didn't like to drive after dark. Teri's two younger sisters and her little brother were the other passengers. She whispered a prayer: "Lord Jesus, please protect my family."

Just then, as they crested a hill, the family faced an eighteen-wheeler in their lane, passing a small car. Teri pulled her brother close to her and yelled, "Oh, God, help us!"

There was nowhere for the van to go but straight into the truck. Teri turned to check on her sister, sitting behind her. As she did she saw two bright red streaks passing her head—inside the van—and exiting the rear of the vehicle.

There was no crash.

Teri's mom pulled over to check on everyone. Teri, her mom, and her sister all noted feeling heat on the left side of their bodies, sensations that lasted for several hours. Teri is convinced that the truck actually passed through their van. She saw the red streaks; she felt heat on the side of her body where the truck must have been. She knew God had answered her calling on his name with a miracle of protection.

People say that advantage depends on who you know, not what you know. When Mother or Father or Teacher or Pastor or Friend just can't provide the help you need, run to the one whose name is a strong tower; true safety really does depend on who you know.

discussion starters

1. Is there value in having a "good name"? Explain.
2. Look up Hebrews 13:5–6. Does this promise in God's Word mean you'll never be afraid? What can you depend on when you are afraid?

lifeline

When you need protection, *call* out to God by name.

He who answers before listening—that is his folly and his shame.

—Proverbs 18:13

60. mistaken hearing

In his book *All Creatures Great and Small*, veterinarian James Herriot recalls his first days in animal practice. James worked for a man named Siegfried Farnon, who had little patience and even less attention for what others were saying. Often Siegfried got in a hurry in the mornings and sent James off to the wrong farm. But one time it happened to Siegfried himself.

James had just taken a call from a farmer whose sheep had died and needed a postmortem examination. Siegfried decided to go along and did the driving. But halfway through the trip, he seemed to make a wrong turn. When James tried to correct him, Siegfried insisted that the farm they were headed for was the right one. James decided to let him discover the error for himself.

When they arrived, Siegfried approached the farmhouse door and asked the bewildered wife for a sharp butcher knife. After several minutes of feverish whispering inside, a little girl was pushed out and presented Siegfried with a knife. He declared it wasn't nearly sharp enough and demanded another.

Presently, a second little girl was shoved out with a huge steel knife. Siegfried was satisfied and began sharpening it while humming tunelessly. He then entered the house to ask for the farmer. He found the farmer's wife, with her children hugged to her, cowering in a corner.

Siegfried explained that he was there to do the postmortem operation on the dead sheep and quickly learned he was in the wrong place. Apologies were made, and Siegfried and James set out sheepishly for the right farm.

Unfortunately, not all miscommunications end this lightheartedly. Failure to listen has brought far more serious results, from schoolyard fights to all-out wars. It's easy to get wrapped up in our own lives and accidentally disregard the needs and concerns of those around us. Because we are Jesus' followers, it's doubly important that we truly listen to those around us. The underlying messages of their words may signal a need for help or prayer. Paying attention to people will reflect the heart and wisdom of Jesus.

discussion starters

1. How can you better listen to others?
2. What can you do to improve your listening skills?
3. Why is it foolish to become wrapped up in your own business and ignore what others say?

lifeline

Get together a group of people and play Telephone. **Sit** in a circle and have one person think of a sentence and whisper it in the next person's ear. **Pass** the sentence around the circle until it arrives back to the first person, then compare the two sentences. **Discuss** the importance of listening carefully to others so the message stays intact. How does this apply to the message of the gospel?

The first to present his case seems right, till another comes forward and questions him.

—Proverbs 18:17

61. two sides to every story

On July 27, 1996, an explosion rocked Centennial Olympic Park in Atlanta, killing one person and injuring more than a hundred others. The casualties would have been greater had not Richard Jewell, a security guard, located the bomb before the blast and notified police. Jewell was proclaimed a hero by the media—for a while.

Not long afterward, the local newspaper broke a story implicating Jewell in the bombing. "FBI Suspects Hero Guard May Have Planted Bomb," the headline glared in bold type. Jewell looked on helplessly as newspapers and television newscasts nationwide picked up the story. Experts were interviewed, with psychologists suggesting Jewell fit the personality profile of a lone bomber. Journalists researching his background painted him as a law-enforcement wannabe who might have planted the bomb out of frustration over his stalled career. For three grueling months, Jewell endured an onslaught of negative media attention. Ironically he was never arrested or formally charged with the bombing. In the minds of many Americans, however, he was guilty. There certainly seemed to be enough evidence.

Yet after eighty-eight days, the FBI called off its investigation of Richard Jewell, expressing "regret" for the incident. His ordeal was over at last. Or was it? Now he faced the task of restoring his tarnished reputation. It would take some time.

It's easy to rush to a conclusion when you have only some of the facts, isn't it? Tyler, age fifteen, discovered several dollars were missing from his bedroom one day. He quickly decided that his sister, Angela, was the culprit. Questioned about this conclusion, he explained, "It wasn't Mom. It wasn't Dad. That means it had to be Angela!" Alas, Tyler's logic was faulty. Based on limited information (he couldn't find his money) he drew an unsupported conclusion (someone took the money), which led to another conclusion (my sister took the money) and eventually wrong behavior (I'll help myself to some of Angela's money since she took mine). All without having given Angela the chance to defend herself.

God values truth. How, then, can we justify forming opinions based on half-truths? We can't. Before coming to any conclusion, ask yourself:

- Is my information accurate?
- Is my information adequate?

discussion starters

1. In a court of law, why is a trial lawyer given the opportunity to cross-examine the witness?
2. Do you tend to (a) accept what you hear at face value or (b) check out the facts first?
3. Solomon was the writer of today's proverb. Which of his life experiences illustrates this principle? (Hint: Read 1 Kings 3:16–28.)

lifeline

Before drawing a conclusion, *resolve* to hear each side of the story.

An offended brother is more unyielding than a fortified city, and disputes are like the barred gates of a citadel.

—Proverbs 18:19

62. stubborn walls

The city of Tyre, the fourth-largest city in Lebanon, near the Mediterranean Sea, has a storied history and remains one of the more intriguing archaeological sites today.

One of the oldest cities in the world, Tyre was once an island city renowned for its beauty and host to a large commercial empire long before Jesus walked the earth. Maritime trade extended from the city to Northern Africa, across the Mediterranean, and even to Northern Europe via the Atlantic Ocean.

Meanwhile, the invention of the alphabet, later refined by the Greeks, is said to have originated in Tyre. Purple dye was invented there as well, leading to a rich dye trade—and the beginning of the association of the color purple with royalty.

But to archaeologists the most striking aspect of Tyre is its ancient walls. The combination of Tyre's high, fortified walls and its position on the water made it a relatively secure city—not that military powers didn't test that position.

For example, about six hundred years before Christ, Babylon's King Nebuchadnezzar had forces lay siege to the city for *thirteen years*! A few hundred years later, the soldiers of Alexander the Great—no slacker when it came to conquest—stormed the city for seven months with no success. Only by building a causeway from the mainland to the island was he able to send troops up the fortified walls.

Because of its wealth and status, Tyre has been attacked through the years on many occasions—

sometimes even falling to the enemy. But it has never been easy because of those heavily defended walls. Even in modern, war-torn Lebanon, the structures are threatened but still standing.

It's safe to say that few soldiers have ever relished the thought of attacking a fortified city like Tyre simply because of the difficulty in getting past the walls. There's a reason God's Word draws on such intimidating imagery in describing how the offended party in a dispute can become as stubborn as one of those walls—and how difficult it can be to settle a dispute that has long turned bitter.

It's better, no doubt, to handle problems with friends and family before they blow up into something greater. Compared with letting a dispute simmer, settling the matter early can be as easy as walking through an open gate. Perhaps that's a gate you can take advantage of today.

discussion starters

1. Have you ever allowed a conflict to escalate and deepen? How difficult was it to eventually resolve—if you resolved it at all?
2. Have you ever been so angry with someone that you refused to talk or listen to them? How can such an attitude make a situation worse?

lifeline

Pray this week for three specific people who have hurt you in some way that is still unresolved. If God leads you to try to resolve the problem, do so—in a loving, humble way. It might not be easy, but it will be worth it.

A man's own folly ruins his life, yet his heart rages against the LORD.

—Proverbs 19:3

63. playing the blame game

Four summers ago doctors told me I had leukemia. They also told me that the medical procedure I would have to go through within the next nine months would more than likely kill me. Needless to say I did not feel like throwing a party with my friends! I was shocked and real, real sad. It was agonizing to think about saying good-bye to my wife and best friend, Debbie-Jo.

When I talked to God, I did *not* feel it was his fault, and I was not mad at him. All I wanted to know was would he be there when I crossed over to the other side. When I closed my eyes one last time, would I open them in heaven and see his face? God gave me two messages loud and clear: He told me that he was my dad and that he would carry me across the finish line at the end of the race. That's all I needed to hear. I trusted him that day, and I've trusted him each day since for the gift of life.

I've talked to so many kids and adults who blame God for everything! They blame him for their brother who was killed by a drunk driver, as if God made the guy in the other car drunk.

They blame him for the fire that burned their house, as if God was into arson.

They blame God for sin in the world, as if God created sin.

They blame God for difficulties in their lives, as if God can't and doesn't use difficulties to make men and women stronger in their faith and their Christian character.

When people play the blame game they get callous and bitter. When people *trust* God they become thankful in all circumstances. They hate the devil more for the bad things he does, and every day they grow closer and closer to God's heart.

discussion starters

1. What, if anything, have you blamed God for? What did you learn through that experience?
2. Why do people blame God for evils of this world? What is a more accurate way to view God during life's difficulties?
3. Who is really to blame for the evil in this life?

lifeline

Write down the things you have blamed God for. **Ask** God to show you how, in actuality, he loved you and cried with you through that bad experience.

> *A false witness will not go unpunished, and he who pours out lies will perish.*
>
> —*Proverbs 19:9*

64. to tell the truth

One of my greatest adventures came when my oldest daughter, Jamie, and I started a clothing company called White Sands. She was fourteen years old, and the line of clothes was for the junior-high and high-school crowd (juniors' sportswear). The line was marketed to Dillard's, Nordstrom, and a few smaller outlets. We did tie-dyes, knits, shorts, tops, pants, etc., and had the time of our lives marketing, shipping, dreaming, designing, sewing, and doing the other myriad tasks required to make a clothing company happen. Jamie made enough money in three years to help launch Kids Across America—a camp for inner-city kids.

One memorable day Jamie was asked to fly to Hollywood to represent herself and her company on a game show called *To Tell the Truth*. Her challenge on the show was to tell the truth while two sharp teen girls who sat beside her as impostors had the task of lying effectively to fool the panel of four Hollywood stars. The more stars who fell for the imposters, the more money the three girls made.

I was amazed how well the two girls lied! They knew nothing about the clothing manufacturing business, but they didn't blush or blink as they played their roles to mislead the panel on the show.

Are you ever amazed at how easy it is to lie to your parents, your teachers, your friends, and even yourself? What about how skillfully some people lie to you? It's scary, isn't it?

God has a lot to say about lying. It boils down to this: Lying is wrong. No matter how clever the

lie or the liar may be, eventually the truth will be known. God knows already. Lying isn't a game. Any small rewards that come from lying—avoiding punishment, making yourself look better, getting what you want—are hardly worth it in the long run. Lying is a sin with serious consequences: loss of trust, humiliation, punishment—even death (spiritual or physical).

To tell the truth? Best habit you'll ever begin!

discussion starters

1. Are there times when you feel it's much easier to lie than to tell the truth? What are the rewards of lying? How do they compare with the consequences?
2. Have you ever tried to stay out of trouble by lying, only to get in deeper?
3. How do you feel when you discover that someone has lied to you? How do you think God feels when you lie?

lifeline

Ask the Lord today to give you the backbone to always tell the truth. **Determine** to cultivate a reputation for truthfulness.

*A hot-tempered man must pay
the penalty; if you rescue him,
you will have to do it again.*
　　　　　　—Proverbs 19:19

65. enablers

At age sixteen Taylor had matured faster than the other guys in his school. At six feet, two inches tall and with 210 pounds of muscle, he was solid as a rock. His powerful legs sped him down the football field for his many touchdown runs. His muscles rippled in his arms as he brought the basketball down the floor and drove it to the basket for his many twenty-point games. Taylor also had the looks. Girls talked about him a lot, and many longed for a Saturday night phone call and a chance to go out with the heartbeat of Central High.

Amy was elated last September when she became the lucky girl to get such a phone call. Taylor took her to the movies and out for a drive. Taylor's moves with the girls were as skillful as his moves on the football field. He always got what he wanted, or he moved on to greener pastures.

This time, he told Amy, it was different. This time he was in love. Amy bought it hook, line, and sinker. She gave him her virginity and felt horrible the next day. When she told Taylor she couldn't go through that again, he got mad. As he stormed away, he said, "You mean I told you I loved you, and you give me that?"

She felt bad that she had hurt his feelings, so she decided to try again. Maybe this time he wouldn't be so pushy. Anything would be better than getting him upset again.

Amy and Taylor went out for three more turbulent months. Every time Amy tried to stop him, he'd get mad and threaten to break it off.

When Amy became pregnant, Taylor's love grew cold. He told her to go to the abortion clinic to "get rid of the evidence." The day she went in alone to let the doctor take her baby's life, Taylor was off with another girl.

discussion starters

1. What is an enabler? How does rescuing a sinful man only lead that person into greater addiction?
2. Describe what your plan of action will be (whether it regards sex, alcohol, drugs, dependence, or manipulation) when a "Taylor" comes into your life.

lifeline

Think through how you will respond to specific threats, challenges, and temptations before they occur. **Write down** your plan of action.

A sluggard does not plow in season; so at harvest time he looks but finds nothing.

—*Proverbs 20:4*

66. a bountiful harvest

Have you ever heard the story of the ant and the grasshopper? In this famous fable by Aesop, an industrious ant worked long and hard during the summer months to store up food for the winter. He carefully carried many ears of corn to his home. But as the ant toiled, a lazy grasshopper began to mock him.

"Why not come and chat with me, instead of toiling that way?" the grasshopper asked.

"I'm helping to lay up food for the winter, and I recommend that you do the same," the ant replied.

"Why bother with winter?" the grasshopper wondered. "We have plenty now." And he continued to chirp and sing as the ant worked.

However, the first chill of winter air soon came from the north and took the grasshopper by surprise. He watched as the grass wilted and the leaves fell off the trees. Through the blowing winds and swirling snow, the grasshopper made his way to the anthill and watched as the ants distributed the corn and grain they had stored together during the summer. The grasshopper then knew he would suffer the consequences of his poor decisions.

Have you ever succumbed to the warm relaxation of goofing off and then been surprised by the chill of reality setting in? Perhaps you put aside studying for a test or practicing for a sports event and suffered the consequence of a poor grade or performance. Reaping what you sow is a basic principle in the Bible—yet it's often ignored because we don't want to put forth the effort to follow it.

But as followers of Christ, we must not allow ourselves to succumb to a lazy attitude. Next time you're faced with the decision to work hard or procrastinate, consider the consequences of each. While relaxation is necessary and has its place, hard work brings a bountiful, rewarding harvest.

discussion starters

1. How have you suffered from choosing procrastination instead of hard work?
2. What rewards have you reaped from hard work?
3. What good seeds can you sow today? What harvest might you reap from them?

lifeline

Next time you go to the grocery store, *notice* the many items in the produce section. Someone put forth the effort to plant the seeds, take care of them, and harvest the results so people everywhere can have nutritious food. When you're tempted to be lazy, *remember* the hard work of people who supply the produce section, and get busy.

Even a child is known by his actions, by whether his conduct is pure and right.

> —Proverbs 20:11

67. who says?

Travis was an all-conference linebacker for our high-school football team. Having grown up in a soccer league, Travis was also a great field-goal kicker. My greatest memory of Travis' football career was a thirty-five–yard, game-winning field goal that defeated our rival high school in a huge upset. After the game the radio reporter asked Travis how he accomplished such a feat under such great pressure. Travis shrugged and quickly gave credit to the linemen who

blocked for him, the center who made the great hike, and the quarterback who held the ball while he kicked it. The kick was soon forgotten; the humility of the one who kicked it will long be remembered.

Everybody but Jolene knew she was the most "drop-dead gorgeous" girl that ever walked through my son's high-school doorways. Funny thing about Jolene, her looks were far outshined by her kindness toward the outcast students—the ones no one else seemed to care for. The less others cared about a particular student, the more out of her way she would go to make their day with her friendship. Flaunting her beauty was far, far down her list of priorities for life.

"If you've got it, flaunt it!" the old saying goes. An older and wiser saying says, "If you've got it, it's a gift. Give it away!"

discussion starters

1. Why are people who are humble about their gifts so admired?
2. Why is it hard not to draw attention to yourself?
3. Do you know someone who has "distinguished" him- or herself by exceptional conduct? Who and how?

lifeline

Ask the Lord to help you eliminate discrepancies between your beliefs and your behavior.

Do not say, "I'll pay you back for this wrong!" Wait for the LORD, and he will deliver you.

—Proverbs 20:22

68. vengeance isn't yours

On May 27, 2001, missionaries Martin and Gracia Burnham were celebrating their eighteenth wedding anniversary at a resort in the Philippines. Suddenly they were kidnapped by the radical terrorist group Abu Sayyaf. The Burnhams, along with two other hostages, were forced to live in the jungle without warm clothes, food, and adequate shelter for more than a year. Each night they were chained to trees to prevent their escape and were constantly threatened with beheading.

Despite these difficult conditions, the Burnhams remained true to the Lord. They encouraged each other and leaned on their relationship with Jesus to survive. Martin often comforted Gracia by telling her he felt they would get out of there soon.

Martin's prediction came true—though he didn't make it out of the jungle alive. As government forces attacked the Abu Sayyaf camp in a rescue attempt, Martin was struck and killed by stray bullets. Gracia was shot but survived. Amazingly, she maintains a joyful attitude. She is happy for the time she had with her husband, and she works to keep his memory alive through her three children.

Though you've probably never faced anything like Gracia's situation, it's likely you've suffered something that made you want to take vengeance on another person at least once. Perhaps someone you thought was a friend talked about you behind your back, or maybe you got in trouble for someone else's actions. It's natural to want to get even, and it can be extremely difficult to forgive. But God wants you to focus on your own attitude and let him take care of vengeance. After all, he's the ultimate judge, and he will make sure the right punishment is given.

discussion starters

1. How do you handle feelings of wanting to get even?
2. How can you better line up your reactions with God's Word?
3. Why is it important to wait on God and let him take care of vengeance?

lifeline

Ask God to help you give revengeful feelings to him and seek forgiveness toward others instead. Next time you're tempted to retaliate against someone, **write** a letter to God, asking him to resolve the situation.

It is a trap for a man to dedicate something rashly and only later to consider his vows.

—Proverbs 20:25

69. promise made

We all make rash promises in moments of fear, frustration, or lack of understanding. There have been a number of times when I've promised something and later wondered if I had been insane to make such a vow. Even the Bible is full of examples of hasty and unwise vows.

Jephthah of Gilead was a mighty warrior. As he led an army of Israelites to battle the Ammonites, he found himself in a tough position. The Ammonites were powerful and terrifying.

The Spirit of the Lord came upon Jephthah to empower him to lead God's people to win the battle. But when he came face to face with his fierce enemies just a short while later, that didn't seem like enough. In a moment of human weakness, Jephthah thought he could bribe God into helping him. He made a rash vow: "If you give the Ammonites into my hands, whatever comes out of the door of my house to meet me when I return in triumph from the Ammonites will be the Lord's, and I will sacrifice it as a burnt offering" (Judges 11:30–31). God was faithful to deliver his people—in spite of Jephthah's horrible vow—and Israel defeated the Ammonites that day. As Jephthah returned home triumphantly, he remembered his promise. Perhaps he thought one of his servants or even an animal would be the first out the door. But much to his dismay, his only child came dancing out to greet him. When Jephthah saw his daughter, he tore his clothes and began to weep, lamenting his vow.

Jephthah's unwise promise brought him unspeakable grief. In the heat of emotion or personal turmoil, often it's easy to make foolish promises to God. These promises may sound spiritual when we make them, but they'll only produce guilt and frustration when we're faced with fulfilling them. Making spiritual deals only brings disappointment. God doesn't want promises for the future but obedience for today.

discussion starters

1. Have you ever made a rash promise to the Lord and later regretted it?
2. Have you ever tried to manipulate or strike a deal with God? What was it? How did it work out?
3. Do you believe a person can use promises of future good conduct to bargain with God for blessings, help, or other payoffs? Why or why not? How do you think God would prefer us to act?

lifeline

Ask God to forgive you for any rash promises you may have made to him in the past.

The lamp of the LORD searches the spirit of a man; it searches out his inmost being.

—Proverbs 20:27

70. tag! you're it!

Some of my fondest childhood memories are of warm summer nights when all of the neighborhood kids joined together for a spirited game of flashlight tag. After a few minutes of arguing over who should be "it," everyone scattered, leaving one poor kid with a flashlight in the middle of the woods. The tagger counted to fifty, then set out, listening for the rustle of leaves or giggles that would give away someone's position. Eventually one brave soul got the guts to make a mad dash toward home base, and the fun began. If the flashlight's beam hit him, he was out; but if he made it home, he was safe. For a few hours, we all forgot we were scared of the dark and dashed from left to right, trying to avoid the light.

Sometimes we try to avoid God's light in much the same way. We think if we run fast enough, we might be able to avoid his all-seeing, all-knowing light. We dodge around, trying to get where we want to be before he sees us. What we forget is that God's light is much more powerful than a meager flashlight. His light illuminates the entire soul.

We can't hide from that kind of light. King David knew this and wrote about it in his psalms: "Where can I go from your Spirit? Where can I flee from your presence? . . . If I say, 'Surely the darkness will hide me and the light become night around me,' even the darkness will not be dark to you; the night will shine like the day, for darkness is as light to you" (Psalm 139:7, 11–12).

God isn't chasing after us with a small beam in his hand, hoping to catch a glimpse into our soul. His magnificent light brightens every corner of our innermost being. He sees everything we are, and we can't avoid his gaze. Slow down. Quit running, and let the Lord's light lead you in the way everlasting (Psalm 139:24).

discussion starters

1. How does the thought of the Lord's searching out your innermost being make you feel? Why?
2. What do you think the Lord sees when he looks into your heart?

lifeline

Thank the Lord that you'll never have to live in darkness again. **Thank** him for his all-knowing, all-seeing ways. **Memorize** Psalm 139:23–24.

To do what is right and just is more acceptable to the LORD than sacrifice.

—*Proverbs 21:3*

'71. true sacrifice

Throughout the Gospels we see Jesus defending his actions time and time again to the doubting Pharisees. They questioned Jesus in everything he did, finding new ways to condemn him almost daily. To understand why the Pharisees were so rigid, it helps to have a basic understanding of the laws of the Old Testament.

Before Jesus came, people had to make atonement for their sins before God. Sacrifices were instituted through Abraham and Moses—not to confine the Israelites to a life of continual shame but to allow them to present themselves clean and holy before God.

The Pharisees of the New Testament, however, took the Ten Commandments and expanded them to include 613 rules that were to be strictly adhered to. The business of atonement was no longer out of awe and fear of God but out of terror at the consequences the Pharisees invoked.

God's original intention for the Sabbath was that it be set aside as a day to rest and offer glory to him. It was to be a day of praise, when man could spend time basking in the Lord's mercies.

The Pharisees, however, had taken all of the joy out of the Sabbath. Because of their numerous rules, people spent most of their days in fear, not really knowing what to do. The rules actually hindered their ability to worship God.

Then Jesus came, and for the first time, someone dared to defy the Pharisees' traditions. He brought a message of forgiveness and hope, not one weighed down with rules, regulations, and threats.

In Luke 13:15–16, after Jesus healed a crippled woman on the Sabbath, he revealed why he chose to ignore the Pharisees' regulations regarding that day: "You hypocrites! Doesn't each of you on the Sabbath untie his ox or donkey from the stall and lead it out to give it water? Then should not this woman, a daughter of Abraham, whom Satan has kept bound for eighteen long years, be set free on the Sabbath day from what bound her?"

Make sure you don't become like the Pharisees, clinging to rules and regulations and not allowing yourself to be moved by the Spirit. Jesus came that we might be free from the bonds of sin. Allow yourself to be free in his love.

discussion starters

1. Are there some areas in which you may have become a little legalistic and need to surrender?
2. Looking at the verses above from Luke 13, what do you think Jesus' message was to the Pharisees?
3. What is his message to you?

lifeline

Consider your faith. **Ask** God to help you obey him out of joy and love rather than mere obligation.

72. the company of the dead

When Jim was a sophomore in high school, he seemed to have everything going for him. He was a tremendous athlete, good-looking, and popular. He was a Christian, and his faith was well respected by most of his peers.

But during his junior year, Jim began to fall out of the loop. While his friends all went out and partied after the football games, he often returned home feeling lonely and frustrated. So one Friday night, after a particularly thrilling victory, Jim decided to accept a buddy's invitation to join him at a party. He had no intention of drinking or using drugs, but he figured it couldn't hurt just to hang out.

When Jim got to the party, however, he felt awkward being the only person not drinking. He grabbed a beer just to walk around with it in his hand. After a few sips, Jim discovered that he kind of liked the beer. Before he knew it, he had finished it off.

It wasn't long before Jim lost control of himself. After several beers he decided to experiment with the drugs that were circulating around the room. But Jim's body couldn't handle the combination of alcohol and drugs. He died the next morning of alcohol poisoning and a drug overdose.

With drugs and alcohol readily available, the temptation to try them is phenomenal. Beware of the devil. He is cunning, and he's waiting for us to stumble so he can lead us down the path of death.

discussion starters

1. Have you ever strayed from the path of understanding?
2. Have you asked God for forgiveness? If so, have you accepted it?
3. What can you do to make sure you don't lose sight of the path set out before you?

lifeline

The Lord's mercies are new every morning. *Live* in confidence, not in fear, of his awesome love.

He who guards his mouth and his tongue keeps himself from calamity.

—*Proverbs 21:23*

73. out of control

The tiny car wasn't much to look at, but at least it was his. A quick bath couldn't hurt it, he decided. He deposited several quarters into the slot, activating the self-serve, high-pressure car wash. Little did he realize just how high the high pressure was. Soapy water erupted suddenly from the nozzle with more force than he anticipated, ripping the hose from his hand. As he watched helplessly, the runaway hose whipped around wildly like a hyperactive cobra, making loud bangs as the nozzle hit the sides and top of his car. Before he could regain control of the hose, it attacked his windshield. Crrraaack!

Soaked and angry, he managed to turn off the controls. He stared in disbelief at the badly cracked glass. It had taken only a moment for things to get out of control, but once they did, the damage that resulted was long-lasting.

Like the runaway hose, our tongues can easily get out of control and cause significant damage. Perhaps you've been the recipient of someone's harsh criticism or the subject of an unkind rumor. How did that kind of talk make you feel? Hurt feelings aren't the only damage an out-of-control tongue can inflict. Ruined reputations, lost jobs, and broken relationships are often what's left once the verbal dust has settled.

Reckless talkers risk losing friends, offending their bosses, or even turning away someone in need of Christ. Terry, a high-school junior, brought a classmate to his church youth service. As he introduced his guest, the unthinkable happened. A member of the group made comical but offensive ethnic slurs—right to the visitor's face! Terry's guest never returned to that church. Was the desire for a laugh worth it?

Calamity simply means "trouble." If you want to stay out of trouble, guard your mouth. Here are some ways to do that:

- Listen more; speak less.
- Choose your words carefully.
- Break the habit of blurting out anything and everything that comes to your mind.
- Watch the volume and tone of voice you use.
- Use your tongue to build up, not tear down.

Determine today to control your speech by letting it reflect the person who controls your heart!

discussion starters

1. Some people pride themselves in "telling it like it is." What are the consequences of such an attitude?
2. Think of a time when your words hurt someone else. What could you have said instead to avoid causing the hurt?
3. Why is "think before you speak" valuable advice?

lifeline

Commit today's proverb to memory. As a reminder, **write** it on a card and **tape** it to a place you're sure to see it.

> *A good name is more desirable than great riches; to be esteemed is better than silver or gold.*
>
> *—Proverbs 22:1*

74. reputation

My wife Debbie-Jo didn't have the money to buy nice clothes like a lot of her high-school classmates, and yet she was crowned homecoming queen. She was probably the poorest student at Southern Methodist University in Dallas, Texas, where I played football on scholarship and watched her cheer for our football team each Saturday. Her dad was killed when she was four years old, and her mom and stepdad worked like crazy to raise five kids. Very little money was left over at the end of the month for clothing.

But Debbie-Jo was the "best-dressed" girl at Saguaro High School in Scottsdale, Arizona, and the best-dressed girl at SMU because her wardrobe was her reputation and with that she wore the finest clothes every day!

Debbie-Jo never drank alcohol, and when many of the college girls spent the night with their boyfriends, Debbie-Jo *always* went to her own room at night.

ATTENTION Dare Yourself

Your reputation is how other people see you. It is more beautiful than the finest designer clothing when it is good, and when it is bad you can't cover it up even with the most expensive designer clothes.

Boys can ruin a girl's reputation with one evening out and one conversation in a locker room. Boys and girls can ruin their own reputations with one bag of marijuana or one six-pack of beer. Fortunately, Jesus can restore a bad reputation with one prayer of repentance and a couple of years of commitment to follow His ways.

discussion starters

1. What is your dream for your personal reputation?
2. Why is your reputation so important to you?

lifeline

Make a list of five characteristics you think Christ would want you to have as a part of your reputation. **Pray** and **ask** God to help you live out one of these characteristics this week.

Drive out the mocker, and out goes strife; quarrels and insults are ended.

—Proverbs 22:10

75. spreading the flames

One of the most famous disasters in American history began in the most trivial of ways.

One evening in the fall of 1871, following a hot, dry summer that had left water reserves dangerously low, a small fire broke out in a Chicago barn owned by a woman named Kate O'Leary. Although neighbors rushed over to protect the adjoining house from the blaze, high winds fanned the flames, which spread to several houses—and then to more houses. By midnight the fire had moved into the center of the city.

The flames weren't completely extinguished until two days later, by which time the fire had ravaged more than two thousand acres and destroyed more than eighteen thousand buildings. Property damages were $200 million, and although fewer than three hundred people died (a low number for such a brutal, fast-moving blaze) another ninety thousand were left homeless—nearly one-fifth of the city's population at the time.

No one knows for sure exactly how the fire started, but one legend claims that Mrs. O'Leary had left an oil lantern in the barn when she went to feed her cows, and one of the animals kicked the lamp over, igniting the hay—and launching what would become known as the Great Chicago Fire. Oddly enough, her home was one of the only structures in the area not to be burned down.

It's incredible how just a small flame can lead to vast destruction when left unchecked. It's the same for people who allow strife within their family or circle of friends to go unchecked. Much damage can result from just a few harsh words of insult or argument.

God says no problem is too small to address, especially when it involves strife among Christians. When the lamp of insult or argument is kicked down in your life, it's best to put it back on the shelf—not leave it lying in the hay, ready to burn.

discussion starters

1. How can anger flare up into serious problems? Have you ever encountered such a situation?
2. What are some godly ways to handle strife among your friends, family, or church?

lifeline

If you've injured someone with anger or resentment, **make** an effort to talk to that person this week, **apologizing** if you need to.

76. when enough is enough

Listen, my son, and be wise, and keep your heart on the right path. Do not join those who drink too much wine or gorge themselves on meat, for drunkards and gluttons become poor, and drowsiness clothes them in rags.

—Proverbs 23:19–21

Diamond Jim Brady (1856–1917) loved to eat. A restaurant owner called Brady "the best twenty-five customers I ever had." And no wonder. A typical Brady breakfast might include steak, pork chops, eggs, fried potatoes, pancakes, muffins, cornbread, and hominy grits—all washed down with a gallon of orange juice.

Lunch was a bit lighter. It often included two lobsters, oysters, clams, deviled crabs, and beef, followed by a dessert of several pies. (Entire pies, not just slices.) His late afternoon snack consisted of seafood—a heaping platter—and lemon soda.

Dinner, of course, was the big meal of the day. In addition to an appetizer of turtle soup, six crabs, and three dozen oysters, Brady would wolf down six lobsters, two servings of terrapin (a type of turtle), steak, two whole ducks, and vegetables (presumably for health's sake). Dessert was a platter of pastries and, typically, chocolates—two pounds' worth. One can only speculate as to what his bedtime snacks were like.

Brady's legendary appetite was not without its repercussions. Diabetes, high blood pressure, and heart disease plagued him, especially in his later years. Doctors noted that his stomach was six times the size of a normal human stomach. Eventually Brady died from complications of his many diseases.

A millionaire, he had lacked nothing during his lifetime—except moderation.

The moral? Too much of a good thing is a bad thing. Take water, for example. A cupful can quench your thirst; a riptide can pull you under and kill you. So it is with many of the good things in our lives. When done to excess, the good can become our enemy:

- Candy tastes good. But too much brings on tooth decay and weight gain.
- Televised sports offer relaxation. But too much viewing fritters away valuable time and cuts back on family interaction.
- Break the habit of blurting out anything and everything that comes to your mind.
- An after-school job brings in spending cash and teaches responsibility. But too much time on the job can affect school grades and interfere with family mealtime or church attendance.

Are there areas in your life that require moderation? As you make adjustments to your spending habits, appetite, or use of time, you'll discover the benefits of "keep[ing] your heart on the right path." God's way is always the best way!

discussion starters

1. Read aloud the dictionary definition of moderation or moderate.
2. What are some signs that a person's behavior is excessive?
3. Why does God value moderation?

lifeline

Ponder the saying "Less is more." How does it apply to today's proverb?

*May your father and mother
be glad; may she who gave
you birth rejoice!*
                    —*Proverbs 23:25*

77. andy

A few years ago, I visited local nursing homes in an afternoon service project with a group of students. One particular visit stands out clearly in my mind.

Eunice was eighty-two years old, and she was delighted to have the group of students come to visit her at the nursing home. She talked with them for nearly an hour and spoke at length about her dog Spanky who had died years before. She told about her years growing up on a Texas ranch. And finally, Eunice told the students about her son, Andy. When she talked about him, she came alive with pride and love.

"My Andy is so special," she said over and over. "All his teachers always told me he was special."

"What makes him special?" one student asked.

"He just loves Jesus so much," Eunice replied, as though the answer should have been obvious. "And he's so successful. He's changing the world. He's making a difference. Not like some young people these days. Would you like to see a picture of my Andy?"

Eunice reached for a small, framed photograph on her nightstand, and the group leaned in for a look at this exceptional man. They expected to see a strong, handsome man standing somewhere exotic, possibly with a Bible in his hand. Instead, what they saw took them by surprise. Andy was severely handicapped, suffering from cerebral palsy. He sat in a wheelchair, his head tilted to the side, and he wore a crooked smile. How was this man changing the world?

"What does Andy do?" one of the girls asked timidly.

"Why he's a man of God," Eunice responded proudly. "He loves Jesus so much! And he never com-

plains. He's the best boy," she continued. "People see my Andy and want to be better."

Andy wasn't bitter about being born with severe physical defects. He felt no need to prove himself to anyone but his Lord. He obviously had a mother who was intensely proud of his achievements. And for that, he was admired. Live your life in such a way that your earthly parents—and your heavenly Father—will be proud and rejoice in who you are.

ATTENTION Dare Yourself

discussion starters

1. What is your heart's desire in life? Who do you want to become?
2. Do you strive to find favor in the eyes of others, or are you looking to find favor in the eyes of your heavenly Father?
3. How do you make your parents or guardians proud? Are they proud of your obedience?

lifeline

Make a list of the attributes that you know your parents are (or would be) proud for you to model. **Carry** your list with you and **look** at it often. **Strive** to be that person.

Do not envy wicked men, do not desire their company; for their hearts plot violence, and their lips talk about making trouble.

—Proverbs 24:1–2

78. saving grace

How many of us have been disappointed by someone we admired? It's not uncommon to feel let down when sports figures, movie and television stars, or others we admire do something wrong. It's discouraging to hear the weekly headlines of celebrities getting busted for drugs or being caught in moral failure. Even more disheartening is the public announcement of a religious leader's fall.

Why do we care about the break-up of another Hollywood marriage? Why is an evangelist's sin so upsetting? Are these people exempt from the temptations of the world? Of course not! The reason we're affected by these things is because we place people who have fame or wealth on a pedestal.

Many of us long to be famous. But most of us will never become movie stars, professional athletes, politicians, or well-known writers, so we live vicariously through the accomplishments of others.

From the notorious 1960s until the close of the twentieth century, "heroes of the recording industry" brought their drugs, their grunge, their violence, and their sexual depravity to the airwaves of American radio. Their CDs and records sold by the millions. Their followers not only bought their records but also bought their lifestyle. Today many of these "heroes" are in the graves they dug for themselves: Jimi Hendrix, Kurt Cobain (lead singer for Nirvana), "2PAC," and "Notorious B.I.G." Many who worshiped these "heroes" live with regret for the things they've done to their bodies and the pain it caused their families.

The writer of Proverbs 24:1–2 warns us not to envy people who are wicked. We're all susceptible to the same temptations, and we're all fraught with human frailties. It's only by the saving grace of Jesus Christ that we can be rescued from the wickedness that constantly threatens to take over our lives. Don't envy *anyone* else, no matter *who* they are. Instead, see them as God sees us all—sinners in need of his grace.

discussion starters

1. Why are most people interested in the lives of others?
2. What should you do when you see another well-known person fall into sin's trap?

lifeline

Thank the Lord for what he has given you, and **pray** for people who are in influential positions.

79. life in the air

Army chaplains fulfill many duties, but the most important one is being a prayer warrior. Facing life-and-death situations every day gives these men and women ample experience with this role.

Recently one chaplain was assigned to a medical team that took care of the injured after ground-combat operations. But as the group was headed to the site where they would care for the wounded, they encountered small-arms fire. Several of the team members were injured and needed to be evacuated. The chaplain worked quickly to help remove them from the battered helicopter and load them onto a plane. As they took off, enemy rocket grenades fired at them, forcing them to fly evasively.

Finally they arrived in safe airspace and assessed the casualties. One man had been shot in the head and was near death. As the medics worked on him, the chaplain began to pray. He touched the man's head and sought God's help. He asked that the soldier would accept Jesus' love into his heart and that God would give him peace. Though the soldier was weakening, he knew what the chaplain was saying and acknowledged the words with upraised fingers.

Miraculously, the man survived. Within ten minutes his vital signs had improved. He survived the flight and recovered completely except for slight memory loss. He now follows Jesus and attends church with his family, and he's a living testimony of Jesus' love and healing grace.

Jesus came to provide the way for every person to have a personal relationship with him. And he has privileged us with the command to share this amazing love with those around us (Matthew 28:19–20). Jesus' second coming is closer than ever, and many people still don't know him personally. They're headed for spiritual death and slaughter. It's time for you to help guide them into eternal life with him.

discussion starters

1. How are you sharing Jesus' love with those who are headed for spiritual destruction?
2. What can you do now to help military chaplains?
3. Why is it important to minister to those who are trapped in sin?

lifeline

Ask God to give you an opportunity to tell three people this month about how Jesus has changed your life. **Pray** for courage to take advantage of the opportunities he gives you.

80. the tortoise and the hare

"The Tortoise and the Hare" is a well-known fable about a race between a quick-footed rabbit and a slow-moving turtle. As the race begins, the hare ridicules the turtle's slowness. The turtle simply sets his face in determination and continues down the path toward the finish line.

The rabbit gets so far ahead of the tortoise that he decides to take a little break and catch his breath. As he relaxes in the warm sun, the rabbit falls asleep.

Some time later the tortoise comes plodding by and sees the sleeping rabbit. Shaking his head at the overly confident hare, the tortoise continues to push his way toward the finish line. You know how it ends: The painfully slow turtle beats the lazy hare.

The moral of this fable fits well with the moral of Proverbs 24:30–34. Laziness won't win the race. Hard work, perseverance, and discipline bring success. If something takes work, don't give up! Even when others seem to race by you in the same task, keep moving steadily toward your goal. And remember, success doesn't necessarily mean winning the race—sometimes it just means finishing. You don't have to be first; you don't have to be fast; just be faithful and finish.

discussion starters

1. Do you have a particular goal that seems too difficult to achieve? What can you do to achieve success in that area?
2. Are you more like the tortoise or the hare? Explain.
3. What consequences of laziness have you observed in your own life?

lifeline

Ask God to give you the strength to persevere through whatever race you may be running in life. **Lean** on him as you make your way to the finish line.

By forbearance a ruler may be persuaded, and a soft tongue breaks the bone.

—Proverbs 25:15 NASB

81. a soft tongue

Yesterday I picked up my ringing phone—as I have been doing for thirty wonderful years of working with kids—and I heard the anxious and stressed voice of a high-school girl on the other end.

"My parents don't understand anything! No one understands where I am coming from. They act like they don't even care!" her voice screamed with great anger.

"What's wrong, Melody?" I asked.

"I hate my youth group, and I want to go to John's youth group. It is so much better than mine it isn't even funny. I'm so upset with my parents, but they won't even listen to me . . ."

Melody couldn't fill my ears with enough anger!

Proverbs says, "A gentle answer turns away wrath" and "A soft tongue breaks the bone."

I really don't think Melody's angry, loud approach with her parents was very persuasive. Do you suppose that she and her parents would ever come to an understanding through her ranting and raving?

Mary, on the other hand, came to me after our Young Life Club one night several years ago. "Joe, I am happy and sad."

"Tell me why you're happy," I said.

"I joined your church," she replied.

"Tell me why you are sad," I continued.

"My parents want me in a different church. My mom wants me in hers, and my dad wants me in his."

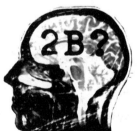

"So, nobody goes to the same church," I said.

"No, we never have," Mary said sadly.

I finally advised her, "Mary, why don't you go to them and gently tell them you'll submit to whatever they say. But softly tell them how good your new church is, and then let God speak to you through your parents."

The next Sunday I was late to church and took a seat near the back of our sanctuary. Sitting next to me was Mary and an older man and woman.

I leaned over to her and whispered, "Mary, who are these two people sitting by you?"

"They're my mom and dad."

"I thought they went to different churches."

"They *did*, but when I approached them softly and with a submissive spirit, they said if my new church taught me to behave like that, they wanted to join that church too!"

discussion starters

1. Why does a gentle answer turn away wrath?
2. Why is a soft tongue more effective than a raging tongue?
3. How can you be more effective in conflict you are experiencing?

lifeline

Memorize this verse: "A gentle answer turns away wrath, but a harsh word stirs up anger" (Proverbs 15:1).

Ask God to bring it to your mind the next time you need it.

If your enemy is hungry, give him food to eat; if he is thirsty, give him water to drink. . . . And the LORD will reward you.
—Proverbs 25:21–22

82. bridge to friendship

Two years after the bombing of the World Trade Center in New York City, a team of Christians from America set out to take food to Iraqi refugees. Their mission was to bring hope and reconciliation to those who had been displaced due to the war in Iraq. They originally had planned to go to Baghdad, but security issues diverted them to Jordan, where an estimated half million refugees lived.

How would they be received? Would Islamic leaders prevent their contact with the people who needed help? Would they be targeted for destruction simply because they were American? Or Christian? Their venture had risks. They knew that radical Islamic fundamentalists would view them as enemies.

Working with local charities, the American volunteers delivered food to hungry families. They also delivered diapers and other baby items to an Islamic women's center and took food and supplies to a nearby orphanage. As they became acquainted with the Iraqis, they gained insight into the culture and personal lives of the people. They listened and wept with mothers who had lost sons and husbands in the fighting. They answered questions when asked about their faith.

One Iraqi translator admitted that he had doubts about how he would relate to the group. But after he saw the unconditional love and acceptance demonstrated by the Christian team, he said, "I feel like I'm with my people." The barriers and stereotypes had been broken.

Offering to meet a practical need can often be a bridge to understanding and friendship. It's a wise way to end hostilities and demonstrate a desire for peace. A gift can go far in injecting God's love into a hateful, fear-charged situation.

People who dislike you, oppose you, or in some way take on the appearance of enemies may be starving for more than food or water. They may need acceptance, appreciation, and understanding. When you give to feed these inner hungers, you disarm your enemy. Nothing is sweeter than the reconciliation that follows.

Fear and prejudice can keep people apart. Someone has to make the first move to break down those barriers. God's blessing awaits the person bold enough to take that step.

discussion starters

1. What are some reasons people become enemies?
2. What practical steps can be taken to restore broken relationships and bridge misunderstandings?

lifeline

Ask God to show you how to build a bridge to someone outside your circle of friendship. *Be willing* to take the first step.

Like a trampled spring and a polluted well is a righteous man who gives way before the wicked.

—*Proverbs 25:26* NASB

33. corrupted by friendship

He was the point guard on his high-school basketball team and star quarterback of the football team, and he knew his Bible better than almost any kid in school. He had memorized great portions of Scripture and seldom missed a Sunday in church. He was, without a doubt, one of the most well-liked kids in his class.

But he didn't always live out what he knew. When he was in seventh grade, he had met two wild friends on his football team, and the friendship prospered through high school. As the threesome grew up, they won football games together, partied on weekends together, chased girls together, and got in trouble together.

The boy who called the plays in the huddle wasn't strong enough to call the plays with his two friends. They called the plays for him. The plays they called asked him to run out of bounds—way out of bounds.

A beautiful girl came along with a need to do whatever it took to get him to like her. Her reputation was loose, and he knew it. Thinking in the beginning that he'd get her closer to God, he found out that she led him closer to the pit. The mistakes he made with her he'll regret for a long time to come.

Jesus, knowing our glaring weaknesses, rightly said, "Be not unequally yoked to an unbeliever" (see 2 corinthians 6:14). He knew that a fast oxen and a slow oxen yoked side by side could not pull a plow. He also knew that a follower of Christ can't pull his weight yoked to one who follows the devil.

More Christian kids than you could write on all the pages of this book have gotten drunk, high, pregnant, and in serious trouble because they didn't listen to God's words of caution: "Like a trampled spring and a polluted well is a righteous man who gives way before the wicked."

discussion starters

1. Where is the one place you should take a friend who doesn't follow Christ?
2. Why is it so much harder to lead a wicked man to Christ than to lead a good man to the devil?
3. What is so bad about a "trampled spring" and a "polluted well"? How are they like a "righteous man who gives way to the wicked"?

lifeline

Consider your friends. Are there any you need to "unyolk" yourself from? **Ask** God to help you do what is best.

Like a city whose walls are broken down is a man who lacks self-control.

—*Proverbs 25:28*

84. controlling myself

Roy Johnson figured he had done pretty well on his driver's exam. With a sense of accomplishment, he pulled the car to a final stop—or, more correctly, a near stop. As he applied the brakes, his foot slipped onto the accelerator. His vehicle, in turn, slipped over the curb—and into the plate-glass window of the Oakland Department of Motor Vehicles. The examiner, who was in the passenger seat, chose not to give Johnson a passing grade. Why? Roy had lost control.

When you're out of control, even for a moment, the worst can happen.

For Derek, an A student, it began as a minor disagreement with his high-school teacher. Derek got too angry too fast. Ordinarily he kept his emotions in check, but this time his anger flared as the exchange of words escalated. Before he knew it, the unthinkable happened—he'd threatened his teacher. Although he hadn't meant it, Derek had to face the consequences of his threat—two weeks' suspension. Derek had lost control.

If we allow our circumstances to dictate our behavior, we run the risk of losing control. Thus, Jon responds to an unfriendly punch on the shoulder with several punches to the jaw. When an angry motorist makes an obscene gesture, Chelsea immediately responds in kind. The church youth group holds a pizza social, and Jared wolfs down sixteen slices of thick-crust supreme. In each of these cases, the individual's lack of self-control opens the door to serious consequences.

What kinds of consequences? Let's come up with a likely ending to each of the above incidents. Jon, the puncher, quickly finds himself part of a knock-down-drag-out brawl resulting in several students' suspensions, including his own. Chelsea? Her retaliatory gesture sparks a fit of road rage on the part of the angered driver, who forces her off the road and into a ditch. As for Jared, the pizza aficionado, he leaves the youth social green, bloated, and miserable, spending much of the night saying good-bye to all his pizza.

In Bible times high, thick walls were a city's primary means of protection. If those walls were broken, an enemy could plunder the city virtually unhindered. Likewise, when our personal walls of self-control are broken down, the enemy of our souls is free to wreak his havoc. Are you keeping yourself protected?

discussion starters

1. Are there any areas of your life in which you lack self-control?
2. Some people explain their misbehavior by saying, "I just couldn't help myself." How would you respond to their explanation?
3. What are the benefits of practicing self-control?

lifeline

The key to self-control is Christ's control. **Give** him control of your life today!

85. finding the strength

The day started out like any other. Tim got up early and read his Bible, then after a quick breakfast he headed out for his morning run. He was training for his second marathon, and he looked forward to the workouts. As he rounded a sharp corner, he noticed a car's headlights coming toward him. Tim jumped into the grass to get out of the way—but it was too late. The driver, not paying attention, swerved off the road and plowed into him. From that moment on, Tim's life was changed.

When the doctor told Tim he would never walk again, he didn't believe it. Every night Tim's wife massaged his numb legs while he tried desperately to move them. As the months passed and his legs began atrophying, Tim fell into depression. His leg muscles grew smaller each day, and his spirits continued to sink.

Happily, Tim's story has a positive ending. After many years of counseling and training, Tim overcame his bitterness and anger and went on to win three gold medals in the Special Olympics. Although his legs are useless, his will and his faith have grown stronger.

No one can will paralyzed limbs to work. Neither can a fool give a proverb meaning. A fool is one who lacks wisdom and discernment—one who speaks without understanding what he or she is saying. All of us are born fools. Not one of us can gain wisdom or discernment on our own. We're all spiritually lame. But like Tim, we have other means of finding strength. Don't quote a proverb unless you understand its meaning—especially its meaning for you. Find your strength in the wisdom of the Almighty.

discussion starters

1. What are some spiritual exercises you can do to strengthen your faith?
2. How does this proverb speak to you?

lifeline

Ask God to give you the wisdom and discernment you need to overcome spiritual handicaps.

As a dog returns to its vomit,
so a fool repeats his folly.
                    —Proverbs 26:11

86. addicted

The average teenage girl who goes to an abortion clinic returns three to five times, according to a woman I know who used to operate five abortion clinics in Dallas, Texas.

A teenage girl told me that she honestly didn't know anyone who drank who doesn't drink too much. Many kids have told me that drinking and morals slide down the same slippery slope of sin, side by side.

Tim smoked marijuana once and swore he'd never do it again. The second time he felt guilty, but he did it anyway. After the third time, he quit thinking about not doing it. He did LSD only once. The drug drove his mind so crazy that he went out and killed himself.

A seventeen-year-old friend of mine in Kansas City was under a lot of stress at home. Her friends told her that by getting high her problems would go away. When she came down from her high, her problems were still there. Now she had another problem. She was a user who wanted to try it again. She ended up in a rehab clinic and almost lost her life.

A dog will return to his vomit, but that's because he's a dog! Dogs don't reason. Dogs don't fear addiction. Dogs can't read newspapers, magazines, and books about the matrix of sin.

Jesus said, "If any man sins, he becomes a slave to that sin" (see John 8:34). Sin is addictive. One beer leads to six. Six beers lead to trouble.

Heavy kissing and petting lead to intercourse. Intercourse leads to pregnancy, disease, and regrets. Marijuana leads to psychological addiction and often to heavier drugs. Pornography leads to a lifestyle of uncontrollable lust.

Fortunately, ever so fortunately, falling in love with Jesus can break a bad habit and remove the guilt of a young man or woman's sin. "If the Son of Man sets you free, you shall be truly free." Truer words Jesus never spoke.

discussion starters

1. How does Jesus—and Jesus alone—keep you from returning to sin?
2. Why is sin so addictive?
3. Is there something in your life that needs to change today?

lifeline

In a private place, **write** down a behavior that is like "vomit" in your life. **Confess** that behavior to a trusted friend or adult. **Ask** God to help you not return to that sin.

Like a madman shooting firebrands or deadly arrows is a man who deceives his neighbor and says, "I was only joking!"

—*Proverbs 26:18–19*

87. sharp bites

Have you ever been bitten by a venomous spider? You'd know it if you had—but perhaps not immediately.

Two of the most common poisonous spiders in the United States are the black widow and the brown recluse. Like all venomous spiders, both devour their food from the inside out, at the same time using their fangs to inject the poison.

The bite of the black widow can cause muscle cramping, nausea, vomiting, and breathing difficulties, and about 1 percent of all bites result in death. The brown recluse's venom causes tissue damage, destroying cells at the point of contact, along with the usual spider-bite symptoms such as fever, nausea, and achy joints. Both bites eventually become very painful.

But here's the catch—many people, especially those who get bitten while reaching under something, don't even realize they've been chomped by a spider at first, because the initial bite doesn't hurt. It's not until later that the affected area becomes painful and inflamed.

Many people have been awakened by a sharp pain on their hand or face from a spider bite; they didn't feel the bite when it happened but they certainly do now. In either case the delay can give the venom time to work in stealth, creating a situation that can be tragic for people who are allergic to spider bites.

Come to think of it, that's often the way cruel jokes and teasing can affect someone. Thoughtless words are vollied back and forth, perhaps never even intended to be harmful, and the victim of the teasing tries to laugh it off. But later, alone and in quiet, those words can sink in—and bite hard.

It's obvious why God's Word compares cruel humor to deadly arrows—it can pierce the heart as easily as a real arrow pierces skin. But the spider analogy is just as apt, since the cumulative effect of teasing—especially when it's endured over a long period of time—builds gradually and hurts more the longer it festers.

Consider the words you use when you think you're just joking around. The pain they inflict can last longer than a spider bite, and emotionally they can be as deadly as arrows.

discussion starters

1. Have you ever gone too far in joking around and hurt someone's feelings? Once you realized it, what did you do? Does peer pressure play a role in giving others a hard time?
2. How does it make you feel when you're unfairly teased about something? Do you feel the urge to fire back? How do you handle such a situation?

lifeline

Write the words *joy, humor,* and *teasing*—three types of laughter—on a piece of paper. Then **write down** the positive and negative aspects of each. **Ask** yourself whether it's ever necessary to be mean to someone else, even in jest.

88. set up for a fall

Things were looking rough for General George Washington and his soldiers. It was the day after Christmas in 1776, and Washington's Continental Army had endured a relentless series of attacks by the British Army and its allies. The colonial troops fighting for freedom from Britain were exhausted, stricken by disease and hunger, and facing bitterness and even desertion by some soldiers.

As Washington's men tried to regroup in Buck's County, Pennsylvania, just across the river in Trenton, New Jersy, fourteen hundred Hessian soldiers—Germans fighting on the British side—were having a better time of it. Or so they thought. The war was going well for them, and after drinking and partying through the holiday—and no doubt boasting of their exploits—the Hessians were completely unprepared for a decision by Washington that would echo through the ages.

Washington knew the time was right to make a bold move. He led a group of his men on a mission across the Delaware River under cover of night and attacked the sleeping Hessians. It turned out to be more of a rout than a battle, as about a hundred Germans were killed and another nine hundred taken prisoner. The American casualties? Four injured and only two dead—both from cold and exhaustion on the march to Trenton, not in battle.

The surprise victory was a morale booster for the Continental Army, and the colonials would win more victories on their way to winning the Revolutionary War—all because they took advantage of an overconfident bunch of soldiers who felt they could take the day off to toast their success.

It's an old story and one often repeated, but it's a lesson worth noting. Few things can bring a quicker downfall than resting on yesterday's accomplishments and assuming they'll bring you victory tomorrow. Boasting about success not yet attained is risky—especially if you can't see the big picture. And overconfidence tends to make that picture mighty blurry.

God wants you to strive for success in every way—every day. But he'd rather you let someone else keep score. Don't be so sure of yourself that you let down your guard and let your spiritual enemy win the battle.

discussion starters

1. How can you apply the lesson of the Hessians to spiritual overconfidence? What is the danger of letting down your guard spiritually?

2. What is the difference between taking normal pride in your achievements and becoming boastful? How difficult is it to walk that line?

lifeline

Consider some of your achievements in school, church, and your family life. Then **think** about the people—and God—who helped you achieve them. **Train** yourself to focus on being appreciative to others, not on yourself.

Let another praise you, and not your own mouth; someone else, and not your own lips.

—*Proverbs 27:2*

89. aren't i something?

The toga-clad crowd cheered wildly amid the thunder of horses' hooves and blur of chariot wheels. A scene from *Ben-Hur?* No. It was the Olympic games in A.D. 67. By all accounts, it was a shameful spectacle, as evidenced by the unorthodox chariot race.

All eyes were on the celebrity contestant as he maneuvered his vehicle clumsily around the track, dust swirling everywhere. Clearly he didn't know what he was doing. The contestant lost his balance; the audience gasped as his 360-pound frame hit the ground with a thud. As if falling off his chariot weren't enough to disqualify him from the event, he chose not to complete the entire course. Incredibly, he was declared the winner! What was happening here?

The contestant was the infamous Roman emperor Nero, whose legendary cruelty was matched only by his pride. In an effort to bolster his ego, he had decided he would enter—and win—several Olympic events. No one dared argue with the emperor, neither the judges he bribed nor the personal cheering section, five thousand strong, that he insisted attend each event. So desperate was Nero for the approval of an audience that he invented new Olympic events to showcase his talents in music and drama, which were minimal. All told, he "won" six events (the equivalent of six modern-day gold medals) and a lot of accolades, forced as they were.

Did it occur to Nero that the "praise" he received for his efforts rang a bit hollow? It appeared to come from the lips of his subjects, but in reality it was only his own. Nowadays few people have means or the nerve to purchase their own fan club as the emperor did. Yet like Nero, some individuals insist on boasting about their accomplishments. This aren't-I-something attitude may be good for a momentary ego boost, but according to today's proverb, seeking one's own honor is dishonorable.

There's nothing wrong with receiving affirmation. In fact, you should anticipate positive recognition when you've done well. If you do receive it, accept the praise gracefully. If you don't, avoid giving in to the temptation to brag on yourself. Instead, remember that God sees your accomplishment and takes note of the good you do throughout your lifetime. If you remain faithful in serving him, someday he will award you that highest of all possible accolades: "Well done, good and faithful servant!"

discussion starters

1. Do people tend to like or dislike those who seek their own honor? Why?
2. Is it sometimes proper to draw attention to your own accomplishments? Explain.
3. Recall some Bible characters who sought their own praise. What were the consequences of their prideful attitudes?

Look for ways to praise others.

90. don't be a birdbrain

Mike and Stephanie were a newlywed couple enjoying their first apartment. Not long after they moved in, a bird built a nest on their balcony. Stephanie loved birds, so at first she was thrilled at the idea of a bird making its home where she could watch it up close. But this little bird wasn't very bright. She built her nest in the dryer duct, which not only was disastrous for her but potentially dangerous for the couple. A lot of hot air flows through that duct, and the last thing Mike and Stephanie wanted was dry straw and grass from a nest catching fire inside the walls.

Though they tried to keep the bird out of the duct, she would not be deterred. One morning, without even thinking about the bird, Stephanie turned on her dryer. As she sat down at the kitchen table to eat breakfast, she heard a thud. She looked out the window and was dismayed to find the bird's nest strewn across her balcony! All of the eggs were smashed. Stephanie's heart broke for the little mama bird as she surveyed her loss.

"Well," Stephanie told Mike later that day, "maybe she'll learn her lesson."

Yeah, right. Mike and Stephanie went through that song and dance three times before the bird got the idea. Each time she built a nest in the duct, she lost her babies. She wasn't getting the picture. Mike was still searching for alternative methods of keeping her out when he realized she was gone. After losing numerous chicks, she had gone to find a safer place to build her home.

How often are we like that little bird? How many times does God have to teach us a lesson before we finally learn it? Gives the term "birdbrain" a new meaning, doesn't it?

Don't make the same mistake as the bird. When there's a lesson to be learned, take note and learn it well. Don't be like the simple, who go through hardship after hardship before they finally make a change. Learn your lesson the first time; you'll save yourself a lot of heartache.

discussion starters

1. Have you ever had to learn a lesson the hard way?
2. What did that situation cost you?
3. What steps are you taking to make sure you never have to learn that lesson again?

lifeline

Ask the Lord to bless you with discernment and prudence so you won't keep making the same mistakes.

If a man loudly blesses his neighbor early in the morning, it will be taken as a curse.

—Proverbs 27:14

91. can others tell when you mean well?

You can relate. Finally, it's Saturday and you're sleeping in. But the neighbor's lawn mower roars to life under your window as the first ray of sunlight peeks up over the horizon.

Nothing wrong with the neighbor mowing his lawn. But does it have to be at 6 a.m.? The normally tolerable hum of the mower sounds to your sleepy ears like a 747 landing in the driveway.

It's not personal, but it sure feels personal. Your neighbor is just trying to do a good thing, but he's rather self-absorbed in his presentation. Obviously he set his alarm early to get up and do a good thing, thinking nothing about your being in dreamland a few feet away. He could mow the lawn later, after all.

Timing is important. And it's not rocket science. You may be busting with something great to share, but think about how it will make others feel before you proclaim your great news.

Sure, you're excited that you made the team, but rushing to tell your friend who didn't seems like an intentional insult. Your big brother who has learning disabilities probably doesn't need to hear that you aced another test without cracking the book.

It's great to have good intentions, but it's not enough. "I didn't mean to hurt your feelings" sounds pretty lame when you've been thoughtless in your presentation. Even if your neighbor mowed your parents' yard too, you still wouldn't get to sleep in. Despite his good intentions, you wouldn't feel appreciative.

It's easy to think about what a great thing it is when you're complimenting someone or doing a good deed. But remember that it's not about you. Think before you speak or act so your blessings really bless.

discussion starters

1. Is there a bad time to share something good? Describe such a situation.
2. Why is it sometimes difficult to know when the timing's right?

lifeline

When your timing is insensitive, *go* to the person privately and *ask* for forgiveness. And *ask* God to help you forgive when others hurt your feelings with their good intentions.

*As iron sharpens iron, so one
man sharpens another.*
—Proverbs 27:17

92. partners in the sublime

La Cabana Prison was known in Cuba as the death house. More prisoners died there than in any other prison. It was a place of misery and torture. It was the last place Noble Alexander—imprisoned for his evangelical faith—expected to find a Christian friend. Yet it was there that he met Antonio, a former officer in the Cuban Constitutional Marines, who had become a born-again believer.

To find a Christian brother in that setting was almost too good to be true. But as facts emerged, Noble discovered that he had helped influence Antonio for Christ years before when he gave him a booklet entitled *Steps to Christ.* Now it was Antonio's turn to influence Noble.

"I have a plan," Antonio whispered. In prison such a statement usually translated "escape plan." But that wasn't the case with Antonio.

"Dear friend," he explained, "it is my mission to share the Gospel here in this prison. Will you help me?"

Noble looked around. Prisoners were everywhere—some in cells, some walking the aisles, and others just standing around listening. There was no place for them to go and nothing for them to do.

"How do we begin?" Noble asked.

Antonio didn't answer directly. Instead he began to sing. "At the cross, at the cross . . ." Noble joined in. Soon a third voice joined them. Their mission had begun.

Together, Noble and Antonio started a prison ministry that reached hundreds of inmates.

Although they were persecuted and tortured by Communist guards, they persisted in prayer, praise, and Bible study. They maintained their mission. They stood together, and their faith remained strong.

After twenty years Noble was released. What he left behind was a strong church—and friends who would continue to stand true to their faith because of his example.

When choosing your friends, look for someone who will involve you in worthy projects—someone whose dreams will challenge you to be a better person and to reach for higher goals. Seek out others who will sharpen your vision and take you to a higher level—people who will bring out the very best in you.

discussion starters

1. How have your friends influenced your life?
2. How can you be a positive influence in their lives?

lifeline

Think of a worthy project you can initiate. *Ask* your friends to get involved.

He who tends a fig tree will eat its fruit, and he who looks after his master will be honored.

—*Proverbs 27:18*

93. a reward for your efforts

Frank was an aspiring author, but nobody wanted to publish his book. For five years he'd toiled on the manuscript, working out of the travel trailer he and his wife called home. Things weren't easy. During the day he worked in a factory, bringing in barely enough money to make ends meet. In the evenings he would work on his novel—a Christian thriller—uncertain it would ever find a publisher. Like a painter creating a masterpiece, brushstroke by painstaking brushstroke, he carefully built his plot and characters. Would this story be his masterpiece? None of the half-dozen publishers he'd contacted seemed to think so. There wasn't much of a market for Christian fiction, they felt—at least not the kind Frank was writing.

Eventually a publisher was willing to take a gamble on his novel. At last! The book was published and distributed to Christian bookstores—where it sat. And sat. And sat. Nobody was buying the book. Surely all of Frank's hard work was good for more than just collecting dust. If only someone would read it.

In time, someone did read Frank's book. That someone was Amy Grant. When she held it up at a concert and endorsed it, favorable word of mouth promoted the book more effectively than any marketing campaign could. After eighteen discouraging months, sales of *This Present Darkness*—Frank Peretti's spiritual-warfare thriller—took off. Not only did it top the Christian bestseller list, it helped dramatically expand the market for Christian fiction. The reward for Frank's labors was a long time in coming, but it came nonetheless.

It's easy to become discouraged when you don't see much fruit for your efforts. Perhaps you've scrimped and saved for college or a car but still have little to show for your efforts. Or maybe you've burned the midnight oil studying your chemistry textbook only to pull nothing better than Cs and Ds. It could be that family members or friends you've tried to win for Christ seem as far away as ever from accepting him. Or perhaps that special dream of yours—running a marathon, becoming a playwright, entering the mission field—seems even more unattainable than you'd first imagined. Whatever your situation, hang on! You gain nothing by giving up. Rather, keep tending your personal "fig tree" and leave the results to God. Who knows? The final product just might amaze you!

discussion starters

1. Can you think of a Bible character who experienced discouragement, only to be rewarded later? What can you learn from his or her experiences?

2. How does God reward Christians for doing good? Does he have more than one way of doing so?

lifeline

Don't wait until you see the fruit of your labors to show gratitude to God. He is at work in your life in times of toil as well as times of harvest. **Be thankful** today!

94. a peaceful conscience

Seven-year-old Shelby was at the grocery store with her mom. As they wandered down the aisles for what seemed like an eternity, something caught her eye. It was the most beautiful sight she had ever seen. She was mesmerized by its glitter—drawn toward it, heart pounding in awe. She had seen . . . sparkly stickers!

Shelby was an avid sticker collector. Her sticker book was filled to the brim with Rainbow Bright, My Little Pony, Cabbage Patch Kids, and Scratch-and-Sniff stickers of every kind. But she didn't have any sparkly stickers. And she knew in her heart that was exactly what she needed.

She snatched a package of the childhood gems and rushed over to her mom, explaining in her most dramatic voice how badly she needed those stickers. Much to the little girl's dismay, her mother shook her head no! Her need had been dismissed with hardly a glance. So she thrust the stickers up to her mother's face and resorted to begging, hoping that nagging—combined with the beauty of the stickers—would sway her. But Mom stood her ground, so Shelby sullenly marched back and laid down the precious treasures.

Then she had an idea. What if she just took the stickers? Nobody would know. She crept back to the sticker aisle. Seeing no one, Shelby grabbed the package and stuffed it in her jacket.

As mother and daughter drove home from the store, guilt and fear suddenly gripped Shelby. She knew she had done wrong, but she couldn't back out now. She decided to look at the stickers to remind herself of their beauty. Slowly she pulled them out and stared. Tears welled up in her eyes. The stickers didn't seem so beautiful anymore. Shelby looked away. She had to rid herself of the guilt. She decided to give the stickers away as soon as she got home.

Unfortunately—or perhaps fortunately—she didn't make it home. Shelby's mom caught her with the stolen stickers and immediately took her back to the store. She made her daughter talk to the manager and apologize for what she'd done. Shelby was humiliated.

But now, years later, Shelby says she's grateful to her mom for teaching her that lesson. "Once I had given the stickers back and apologized, I felt better. A burden had been lifted."

Confession does that. It releases the burden of guilt that weighs heavily on our shoulders. And with that release comes amazing peace.

discussion starters

1. Why do you think God chooses to be merciful to the person who confesses?
2. Even though Shelby was a child, she not only knew how to steal and lie but how to try to justify herself. What's the danger in trying to rationalize or justify our sins?

lifeline

Give yourself the peace of a clear conscience. *Confess* your sins to God today.

Bloodthirsty men hate a man of integrity and seek to kill the upright.

—Proverbs 29:10

95. evil hates good

In Sri Lanka, a country hostile to Christianity, several women who were building a fence on church property experienced severe harassment at the hands of a non-Christian religious official. That night a band of men tore down the fence, awakened the women, and assaulted them. Next the women were brought to police and accused of made-up crimes. They eventually were cleared of the charges, but one week later the church building was burned.

In California, Mission Viejo High School refused to allow a student-led Fellowship of Christian Athletes club to meet on its campus. "Our concern is some of those interests [of noncurricular clubs] represent opinions and beliefs that we feel are counterproductive with respect to our students," the district superintendent stated. A state appeals court ruled the Christian club ought to have access to the school facilities. How did the school board respond? By eliminating not only FCA but twenty-nine other noncurricular clubs as well. When angry parents complained about the dismantling of the clubs, a board member replied, "Blame the Christians."

For a class project in Pennsylvania, a Christian high-school student debated a nonbelieving student on the merits of Creation versus evolution. Evaluating the debaters' content and technique, a classmate opposed to the creation viewpoint scrawled profanity on the Christian's scorecard.

The above accounts all involve persecution of Christians, some severe, some subtle. Troubling as such incidents are, they underscore an important point: Evil hates good. Doing the right thing won't necessarily make you popular with the world at large. Jesus advised his disciples, "If the world hates you, keep in mind that it hated me first. . . . If they persecuted me, they will persecute you also" (John 15:18, 20).

Does the thought of persecution upset you? Don't let it. No matter how great the opposition Christians may face, God is greater! Nothing escapes his notice. He can use even the harshest of situations to further his kingdom.

The next time you face opposition for your beliefs, don't become frightened, angry, or discouraged. Rather, bring to mind Jesus' words: "In this world you will have trouble. But take heart! I have overcome the world" (John 16:33).

discussion starters

1. Why do you think individuals are opposed to Christianity in general and Jesus in particular?
2. What resulted when believers in the book of Acts faced severe persecution? (Hint: Read Acts 8:4.)
3. What does this teach us about persecution?

lifeline

Don't be tempted to water down the message of Christ in order to get people to like you. *Be willing* to stand up for Jesus!

Many seek an audience with a ruler, but it is from the LORD that man gets justice.

—*Proverbs 29:26*

96. divine power

Dave was tried and convicted for murder when he was eighteen years old. His sentence was just and fair in the eyes of the law, but that didn't make his life in a Texas prison fair or pleasant.

Dave's life before prison taught him that only the toughest guys survived. He learned to use power and aggression to even the playing field. In prison he learned that showing emotion other than anger and retribution meant a life sentence of being bullied, if not killed.

Then Dave met an "outsider" who became his friend. Dave's new friend introduced him to Christian love, real respect, and a just power. Eventually, Dave asked Jesus to be his Savior and friend.

Believing in Jesus changed Dave's heart, but the personality change took a little longer. When he wanted to have church, he bloodied mouths with a toilet brush to intimidate the tough guys into cooperating. When he wanted to quit cussing, he asked his cellmate to hit him every time his speech wasn't pure.

But as Dave experienced true freedom, even behind the prison bars, he began to understand that power could be used for good. He learned to trust God's plan, even when circumstances seemed to require physical power. Dave's life of peace influenced even the toughest prisoners. Word got around, and new inmates were told, "If you want to survive, look up Dave. He'll help you."

God used Dave in his prison circumstances, but he also had plans for him outside of prison. Rather than having to serve his full term, Dave was released after only eight and a half years.

Now more than two thousand people attend the church Dave pastors—and there have been no reports of his chasing people to church with a weaponized toilet brush. When the odds were against him, Dave trusted God to work things out rather than taking matters into his own hands.

Life isn't fair, and you can't make everyone play fair. Sometimes you may even give in to the temptation to exercise power. Instead of getting angry or seeking your own justice, get in the habit of asking God, "What are your plans for this situation?" Wait for his answer—it will be far better than you can even imagine.

discussion starters

1. Are you in a situation where you've "gotten what you deserve"? Does that make you feel like no one can make right out of what you've done wrong, including you?
2. Why is relying on God's power instead of our own physical strength or emotional power so scary?

lifeline

When the odds are against you or you've gotten what you deserve in man's eyes, **ask** God to use the situation in your life for something good rather than seeking imperfect justice for yourself.

I am the most ignorant of men; I do not have a man's understanding. I have not learned wisdom, nor have I knowledge of the Holy One. Who has gone up to heaven and come down? Who has gathered up the wind in the hollow of his hands? Who has wrapped up the waters in his cloak? Who has established all the ends of the earth? What is his name, and the name of his son? Tell me if you know!

—Proverbs 30:2–4

97. audacious questions

God, why did you let me injure my knee in the first football game of the season?

> God, why did you take my girlfriend away?
>
> God, why did you let my parents divorce?
>
> God, why don't you find me a boyfriend?
>
> God, why am I hurting so badly right now?
>
> God, why . . .

In Proverbs 30 Agur, son of Jakeh, shows the ignorance of humans by asking a series of unanswerable questions.

Who can understand the mind of God? (Answer: *no one!*)

A God who is small enough for us to understand isn't big enough for us to worship!

As you know from earlier devotions in this book, I have a blood cancer called leukemia. The prospect of dying a horrible death doesn't excite me in the least, but I have never asked God why because, like Agur, I'm absolutely positive that God is a lot smarter than I am. And even though his ways are not my ways, I trust that his ways are higher, wiser, and better than mine.

Who am I to question God?

My only option is to trust him and thank him, knowing down deep in my heart that his love is all I need and that his grace and eternal life is all I want.

discussion starters

1. Why do we question God when things go wrong?
2. When we ask why, are we looking for answers, or are we looking for a fight? Explain.

lifeline

Gain the confidence to answer tough spiritual questions by *leaning* on the steady and solid foundation in the Word of God.

Speak up for those who cannot speak for themselves, for the rights of all who are destitute. Speak up and judge fairly; defend the rights of the poor and needy.

—Proverbs 31:8–9

98. taking a stand

It's amazing to think that schools in America were segregated by law only fifty years ago, forcing black students to attend inferior schools as compared with those of their white peers.

Then the Supreme Court ruled in the 1950s that all public schools must accept students of all races. But that didn't go over so well in some districts. In Little Rock, Arkansas, the school board decided it liked the way things had operated before, so it maintained its all-black school and set strict limits on the number of its students who could transfer into the traditionally all-white school across town. Only nine black students were accepted in 1957, the first year under the new law.

Even that minor concession to equality angered Arkansas Governor Orval Faubus, who had won election on an anti-integration platform. He sent state National Guard troops to prevent the black students from entering the white school, and a crowd cheered them on as they carried out the task.

A court order eventually put a stop to that and allowed the new students in, but they had a rough time. They were pushed around, spit at, and mocked daily. They arrived at their lockers in the morning to find them destroyed, and there were reports of white students throwing flaming wads of paper at them in class.

Eight of the nine black students finished the year, with the one senior among them graduating. But Governor Faubus was enraged at the courts and ordered the shutting down of all the city's public schools, forcing the black students to sit out while their white peers attended private schools. It took another court order to reopen the schools in 1960. Two more of the group known as the Little Rock Nine returned and eventually graduated.

Discrimination still poses problems in America, with blind hatred popping up from misguided people of all races. But it has been a long walk to relative equality, with strides made over the years by brave people like those nine teenagers.

History remembers them well. But Governor Faubus won't receive the same acclaim from most people. God would also condemn his actions, because he shrugged off repeated commands in the Scriptures to defend those who need defending. The governor, sadly, was interested only in himself.

There are plenty of causes for which you can take a stand. But standing up for others—especially the oppressed—has rewards that carry into eternity.

discussion starters

1. What does it mean to you to defend those who need defending? Can you apply this lesson to anyone in your school or church who needs a friend?
2. On a larger scale, what big causes have gotten you excited and made you want to take a stand? Can the actions of one person make a difference? How?

lifeline

Take a quick read through the front section of the newspaper today and **note** how many stories involve people being mistreated or oppressed. **Ask** God to help you treat people as he would treat them.

> *A wife of noble character who can find? She is worth far more than rubies. Her husband has full confidence in her and lacks nothing of value. She brings him good, not harm, all the days of her life.*
>
> —Proverbs 31:10–12

99. nothing but the best

As a small child, I fantasized about treasure hunts. For my birthday my mom would occasionally fill a treasure chest with shiny coins (mostly pennies) and make an intricate, antique-looking treasure map. She'd hide it in an old book strategically placed on the bookshelves of our home. The map would lead to some creative "treasure"—like a ring on a string hidden in a dried-out animal skull, hidden in the fork of a mesquite tree in a field nearby. With the use of a compass and careful pacing, I would be led to the spot of the dig. The details of the hunt were intriguing.

In the days when a five-cent Coke at the movies was a rare luxury, the pennies inside the chest were quite a reward. But even pirates' treasures filled with rubies, diamonds, and gold will never come close to the unmatchable value of a "Proverbs 31 woman."

An excellent wife is of a worth far beyond jewels. She's your hero, your faithful friend, your lover, your pal, your admirer, your Christian role model, your confidante. She represents Jesus well. Her morals are as good as they come. Though I deserved far less, the greatest treasure hunt of my life culminated when I married a Proverbs 31 woman! Though rare, I meet Proverbs 31 women every year by the dozens on the Kanakuk counselors' staff. They come from more than two hundred college campuses coast to coast. Any guy who gets to date or marry one of them is one of the luckiest men alive. The best part about my Proverbs 31 woman is that as the years go by, she becomes more and more of a treasure.

When a Christ-centered guy dates a teenage or college-age girl, his number-one job is to treat her as a Proverbs 31 woman deserves—to love and respect her. A Christian girl who wants a great marriage can't do anything more important than to walk, talk, act, and dress like a Proverbs 31 woman.

"Charm is deceptive, and beauty is fleeting; but a woman who fears the LORD is to be praised" (see Proverbs 3:30).

discussion starters

1. Why does inner beauty transcend outer beauty?
2. How does a girl become a Proverbs 31 woman while she's still in her teens?
3. How can a guy help bring out the best in a girl he dates?

lifeline

Read the whole Proverbs 31 chapter. **List** the qualities of the worthy wife. **Ask** God to help you be or find a Proverbs 31 woman.

Charm is deceptive, and beauty is fleeting; but a woman who fears the LORD is to be praised.

—Proverbs 31:30

100. beauty that never fades

Agnes Bojaxhiu and Naside Saffet probably didn't know each other. They grew up in two different European countries. But in 1931 both young women took a decisive step. Naside entered a beauty contest sponsored by a Turkish newspaper and won the title of Miss Turkey. Agnes entered a convent and took the name Teresa.

Naside sought recognition but failed to win any international contests. Agnes wasn't concerned about fame or fortune, but she eventually received international acclaim for her humanitarian work. The Nobel Peace Prize was among her many honors.

Little is known about Naside Saffet apart from her moment of fame as a beauty queen. Mother Teresa, however, has been elevated to sainthood in the eyes of many. Her ministry to the poorest of the poor in India and other countries has won her a place of respect and admiration. The work she began in the slums of Calcutta now reaches beyond that nation. The little woman in the white sari has become a symbol of compassion and humble service.

Mother Teresa's spiritual journey began when she was only twelve, when the call of God became real to her. Throughout her teen years, she was involved in a youth group at her church and became interested in foreign missions. She decided to join a convent and did so when she was eighteen.

Mother Teresa first taught at a high school in Calcutta. But the suffering and poverty she saw outside the confines of the convent affected her deeply. In 1948 she obtained permission to leave the convent school and start an open-air school for children from the slums. She depended on God to provide whatever funds she needed. In 1950 she was granted permission to start her own order, the Missionaries of Charity. The order's mission was to love and care for those whom everyone else rejected.

Mother Teresa stands out because of the choices she made. She allowed God to speak to her about the needs of the poor; she committed herself to his desires for her; and she walked in obedience where he led. To those she comforted in their dying moments, she was like an angel—the most beautiful person in the world.

True beauty lies in a person's character—not in his or her appearance or wardrobe. It goes much deeper than outward appearances. It involves attitude, conviction, and commitment. A life lived for God and his design will be marked by an inner glow that cannot be duplicated. Such people will be remembered for what they did, not how they looked.

discussion starters

1. What influences in society create an overemphasis on appearance?
2. What character traits make a person beautiful in spirit?

lifeline

Select one positive character trait that you want to develop in your life. **Ask** God to help you make it a reality through daily choices and actions.

Sources

36. Kindness
1. *The Inn of the Sixth Happiness,* DVD, directed by Mark Robson (1958; Los Angeles: 20th Century Fox Home Entertainment, 2003).
2. St. Andrew's Sermons Web site, http://homepages.tig.com.au/~gilbert/sa_web/sa_sermons02_1.htm.

37. Give It Away
1. Jerry Schwartz, "Rich Man Gives Much of Himself to Others," *The Virginian-Pilot,* November 28, 2003.

68. Vengeance Isn't Yours
1. Gracia Burnham and Dean Merrill, "In the Presence of My Enemies," *Today's Pentecostal Evangel,* (August 17, 2003), 15–18.

76. When Enough Is Enough
1. Gourmandizer Web site, "James 'Diamond Jim' Brady," http://www.gourmandizer.com/ezine/brady/.
2. "Diamond Jim Brady Biography," http://allsands.com/History/People/biographyjimbr_spz_gn.htm. Copyright 2001 by PageWise, Inc.
3. Fascinating Facts Web site, http://www.geocities.com/Tokyo/Pagoda/6917/fascinat11.html.

82. Bridge to Friendship
1. Joni B. Hannigan, "Iraqi refugees receive food boxes on 9/11 anniversary," International Mission Board Web site, http://www.imb.org/core/story.asp?ID=973 (September 22, 2003).

92. Partners in the Sublime
1. Noble Alexander, *I Will Die Free* (Boise, Idaho: Pacific Press Publishing Association, 1991), 37–41.

93. A Reward for Your Efforts
1. Gene Edward Veith, "This Present (and Future) Peretti." *World,* 12, no. 23, (October 25, 1997).
2. Christian Teens Web site, "Frank Peretti, Christian Novelist," http://christianteens.about.com/library/blperetti.htm/.
3. BookBrowse Web site, "Frank Peretti Biography," http://www.bookbrowse.com/index.cfm?page=author&authorID=427.
4. PBS Web site, interview with Frank Peretti, *Religion & Ethics Newsweekly* (September 27, 2002), episode 604. http://www.pbs.org/wnet/religionandethics/week604/feature.html/.

100. Beauty That Never Fades
1. Nobel e-Museum Web site, http://www.nobel.se/peace/laureates/1979/teresa-bio.html/, from Nobel Lectures, Peace 1971–1980, (Singapore: World Scientific Publishing Co.).
2. History of the Miss Turkey Web site, http://www.pageantopolis.com/international/Turkey_history.htm.